Proverbs in Irish
Seanfhocail as Gaeilge

Proverbs in Irish

Seanfhocail as Gaeilge

Garry Bannister

NEW ISLAND

PROVERBS IN IRISH
First published in 2017 by
New Island Books
16 Priory Hall Office Park
Stillorgan
County Dublin
Republic of Ireland

www.newisland.ie

Print ISBN: 978-1-84840-590-5
ePub ISBN: 978-1-84840-591-2
Mobi ISBN: 978-1-84840-592-9

British Library Cataloguing Data.
A CIP catalogue record for this book is available from the British Library.

Typeset by JVR Creative India
Cover design by Karen Vaughan
Printed by TJ International Ltd, Padstow, Cornwall

10 9 8 7 6 5 4 3 2 1

When ancient opinions and rules of life are taken away,
the loss cannot possibly be estimated.
From that moment we have no compass to govern us;
nor can we know distinctly to what port we steer.

Nuair a bhaintear dínn tuairimí ár sinsir agus rialacha
beatha, is caill as cuimse ar fad í.
Ón tráth sin amach níl compás cuí againn dár dtreorú
agus ní léir dúinn ach oiread cén cuan ar a bhfuilimid ag seoladh.

— *Edmund Burke*

To my granddaughters
Willow & Lily

Contents

Introduction

The wonderful thing about proverbs is that they are like free radicals—they suddenly appear and disappear in our habits of speech, darting in and out of our habits of thought.

The world of proverbs is dynamic and holds no frozen truths: for every proverb that advises you to do something, there is another on its heels expressing the exact opposite. 'Birds of a feather flock together', and yet 'Opposites attract'. 'Too many cooks spoil the broth', but 'Many hands make light work'. A person 'Out of sight is out of mind', but 'Absence makes the heart grow fonder'.

But surely this is merely a reflection of life itself. Life is inherently full of paradoxes and contradictions. There is very little that we can point to as being absolutely true in all circumstances, for everything in this world of ours depends entirely for its very existence on its relationship to all other things. This is one of the joys of proverbs—they are living echoes of the infinitely large universe of human experiences, which require a great variety of responses depending on the actual circumstance we may find ourselves in.

But, you may reasonably ask, if proverbs reveal only partial truths that depend on circumstances, why do we use them in the first place? Well, there are several reasons why the use of proverbs is so ubiquitous. Firstly, if it is a well-known expression, then we are indicating to our audience that there is a common acceptance for the principle behind our thinking. Secondly, we are indicating our allegiance to a shared set of cultural experiences. And thirdly, there is usually either a clever use of language or some insightful wisdom in the proverb itself which makes the listener or listeners take note. Such expressions as '*Bíonn an t-am ceart gan gó ar chlog nach beo dhá uair sa ló*' ('Even a stopped clock is right twice a day') serve as an excellent example of these qualities—for indeed a stopped clock is probably the most accurate clock possible at precisely two moments during the day. Combined with this wise insight,

1

the proverb also uses rhyme and so demonstrates a clever use of language too. Indeed, even if a proverb is used fairly rarely, it usually rallies a truth that reveals a deep universality in our human experience. So, if proverbs arise due to some commonly shared human experience, then there's good reason for them to be repeated frequently enough to be recognised by large portions of their language community.

But there must be something more that makes so many people remember and use proverbs in their daily conversations with one another. What is it about a proverb that brings it into existence and allows it to get such a grip on our imagination, and what keeps it alive generation after generation? There are a number of possible reasons for this phenomenon, and here are just a few that might be worth mentioning.

Good proverbs are usually colourful, and create vivid images in our minds:

Troid na mbó maol. — 'The fight of hornless cows.'

Ná maraigh an teachtaire! — 'Don't kill the messenger!'

I ndiaidh a chéile a tógadh na caisleáin. — 'By degrees, the castles were built.'

Capall na hoibre an bia. — 'Food is the horse of work.' (or: 'An army marches on its belly.')

Proverbs can also, on occasions, be remembered because they are succinct and because they trip easily off the tongue:

Ní tréad caora. — 'One sheep is not a herd.'

Giorraíonn beirt bóthar. — 'Two shorten the road.'

Is fearr Aifreann ná Ifreann — 'Mass is better than Hell.'

Sometimes proverbs are remembered because they rhyme, or simply sound good. There are many of these amongst the Irish proverbs in this book, such as:

Ná bac le mac an bhacaigh agus ní bhacfaidh mac an bhacaigh leat!
'Do not bother the son of the tramp, and the son of the tramp will not bother you!'

Níl aon tinteán mar do thinteán féin.
'There is no fireside like your own fireside.'

Sometimes new proverbs arrive piggybacking on other, older, well-known proverbs, such as:

Níl aon tóin tinn mar do thóin tinn féin!
'There is no sore backside like your own sore backside!'

'Capall na beatha—an grá.'
'Love is the workhorse of life.'

There are many more reasons why we care to remember proverbs: humour, family language, habits of speech, and—particularly as far as Irish proverbs are concerned—the teaching conventions of our formal educational institutions.

But more importantly, in my opinion, proverbs are like fossils of speech and language. They hold within them, for those who have a keen ear and eye, a fragment of our cultural history that reflects the whole in their very essence. In a large number of older proverbs we discover many clues that lead us to profound truths about the people and the times in which these sayings were coined. For example:

Ag gearradh na bpóiríní (agus cath in aghaidh góiríní).
'Cutting the seed-potatoes (is like waging war on pimples).'

In other words, to cut corners is a poor endeavour indeed. This proverb goes right back to the Great Famine years. In 1847, seed-potatoes were very scarce, so the peasants began to cut whatever seed-potatoes they had available to them in order to acquire larger yields, but this often resulted in little discernable success, and indeed, frequently even more of the crop

3

perished. So, in rural communities, the cutting of the seed-potatoes was, and perhaps still is, viewed as an activity that can only be considered counterproductive.

Ballaí bána roimh thuras fada ('White walls before a long trip') is another interesting proverb from a historical point of view. It refers to the practice of whitewashing cottages as a means of disinfecting them. So, if a person or family were taking a long trip anywhere, or leaving for any extended period of time, this proverb advises those travellers to leave all their affairs in order before they depart.

Ní hé lá na gaoithe lá na scolb is one of my favourite old Irish proverbs. It loosely translates as 'The windy day is not the day for thatching' (or more literally: 'It isn't the day of the wind the day of the scollops'). A 'scollop' is an instrument in the shape of a looped stick that is or was used by the farmer to secure the thatch to the roof of his cottage. No average Irish speaker today would have an inkling of what a 'scollop' actually might be, but yet they would certainly know the proverb's meaning and its correct usage. And why does this particular proverb and others like it continue to be so popular amongst Irish speakers? I'm convinced that it is because proverbs like these are very deeply rooted in the psyche of those speakers from whose culture and social history they have emerged. Even today, when thatching, unless for decorative purposes, is clearly an anachronism, this fossilised word or hapax legomenon is to be found alive and kicking in this frequently repeated *seanfhocal*.

Preface

It is, of course, impossible to produce anything more than a representative selection of the most commonly used proverbs in modern Gaelic, and this modest collection is merely a 'taster' of the vast and rich treasure-trove of aphoristic folk-wisdom, which is still as vibrant today in the modern language as it was when spoken in bygone years.

This book is not confined to purely Gaelic proverbs as that would not provide an accurate portrait of proverb-usage in the modern language. Although the majority of the proverbs in this book have been taken from old Gaelic tradition, there is also a wealth of sayings which have only come into frequent use from the mid twentieth century to the early twenty-first century:

Mé-féineachas	'My-selfness'. This is a play on '*Sinn Féin*', which translates as 'We Ourselves'. This has led to '*Mé Féin*', or 'Me myself', used to excoriate a person who is totally selfish and egotistical.
Níl aon amadán mar sheanamadán	'There is no fool like an old fool.'
Baile, scoil, paróiste!	'Home, school, parish!' This was a quasi-motto hung in GAA clubs in the early to mid twentieth century, signifying the central pillars of Irish society at the time.

Also included are some biblical or religious sayings which are still being used by a small but as yet undaunted minority of Gaelic speakers. For example:

Liomsa an díoltas, arsa an Tiarna.   'Vengeance is mine, saith the lord.'

Leigheas thú féin, a lia úd!   'Heal thyself, physician!'

Súil i gcúiteamh súile...   'An eye for an eye...'

The old, traditional Gaelic proverbs in this collection have been primarily taken from the Munster and Connaught regions, the Ó Dónaill and De Bhaldraithe dictionaries, and other academic sources such as the Seabhac's (i.e. Pádraig Ó Siochfhradha) magnus opus, *Seanfhocail na Mumhan*. The final selection was on the basis of several determining factors:

(i) relevance or usability in a modern context;

(ii) universality—i.e. the transcultural value of the expression;

(iii) frequency of usage—although this generally was already an aspect of the first two factors; and

(iv) cultural curiosity—certain proverbs might not be frequent or even relevant today, but they have a certain curiosity value that reflects an interesting historical or literary peculiarity.

Below are some examples of these four categories:

(i) relevance: *Is maith an scáthán súil charad* ('A friend's eye is a good mirror'). *Bíonn dhá chos ar bhréag ach ní bhíonn ach leathchos ar an fhírinne* ('A lie has two feet, but the truth walks lame'), etc.

(ii) universality: *Lig dom lig duit!* ('Live and let live!'). *Aithníonn ciaróg ciaróg eile* ('Birds of a feather flock together'). *Folaíonn grá gráin* ('Love is blind'), etc.

(iii) frequency: *Níl aon tinteán mar do thinteán féin* ('There is no place like home'). *Is maith an scéalaí an aimsir* ('Time will tell'), etc.

(iv) cultural curiosity: *Tír gan teanga, tír gan anam* ('A country without a language is a country without a soul'). This is a proverb that was instigated by the writer, educationalist and revolutionary Patrick Pearse, who was deeply involved in the language revival movement at the end of the nineteenth and the beginning of the twentieth centuries.

Where appropriate, orthographical changes have been made in certain proverbs. For example, spelling has sometimes been brought into line with modern standard spelling:

Ná beannuigh an t-íasg go d-tiocaidh sé i d-tír.
Ná beannaigh an t-iasc go dtiocfaidh sé i dtír.
('Do not greet a fish till it comes to shore.')

Some archaic or dialect forms are changed, such as:

Cha robh bolg mór fial riamh.
Ní raibh bolg mór fial riamh.
('A fat belly was never generous.')

But others are kept if they are still commonly used in the instance of the proverb itself:

Bheireann (= tugann) an bás blas don bheatha.
('Death gives a taste to life.')

Where one particular type of saying is expressed in many similar ways, only the most common has been represented:

Ní tréad caora.	'One sheep is not a flock.'
Ní seilg breac.	'One fish is not a haul.'
Ní cogadh troid amháin.	'One fight is not a war.'
Ní samhradh fáinleog amháin.	'One swallow is not a summer.'

Also included in this book are commonly used comparisons, such as: *chomh sean leis na cnoic* ('As old as the hills'), *chomh tanaí le cú* ('As thin as a lathe'), *chomh milis le mil* ('As sweet as honey') etc., as well as some familiar blessings and curses.

Some proverbs are repeated when they fall into more than one category, as several do.

Using proverbs in Gaelic is not the same as in English. An English speaker might frequently consider that the continuous use of proverbs was a sign of a lack of originality or simply the clichéd language of a lazy, unthinking individual who likes to resort to rather banal truisms. In the Irish language, however, the proverb is an integral part of the spoken and written language. It is not used merely to support a particular viewpoint or action, but also to pay a certain hidden homage or tribute to those who went before us, and perhaps, in some strange way, refer our utterances to our ancestors for their tacit approval.

Absence (*Díláthair*)

Grá i gcéin grá i gcónaí.
Love far away is constant love.

Géaraítear an grá i bhfad uainn, neartaítear an grá in aice linn.
Love far from us is more acute, love beside us grows in strength.

Nuair a bhíonn an cat amuigh, bíonn na lucha ag rince.
When the cat is away, the mice are dancing.

Seachnaíonn súil rud nach bhfeiceann.
The eye avoids the thing it cannot see.
(cf. Out of sight, out of mind.)

Is glas iad na cnoic i bhfad uainn.
Green are the hills that are far from us.

Ní chuimhnítear ar an arán ite.
Eaten bread is not remembered.

Adversity (*Cruatan*)

Is cairde sinn naimhde saoil sa bhearna bhaoill.
Life-long enemies are friends in the gap of danger.

Is Gael Gall más call.
A foreigner is a compatriot when needs be.

Is éadrom ualach do chomharsan.
Your neighbour's burden is always light.

Nuair a thig cith tig balc.
It never rains but it pours.

Tagann an mí-ádh ar mhuin chapaill ach imíonn sé de shiúl bacach.
Misfortune comes on horseback but limps away.

Advice (*Comhairle*)

Comhairle do chluas chaoch.
Advice to the blind ear.
(i.e. wasting one's wisdom on someone who cannot or will not hear)

Comhairle an chait don mhadra.
The cat's advice to the dog.
(i.e. inappropriate advice)

Comhairle an Earraigh san Fhómhar.
Advice for the spring (given) in the autumn.
(i.e. advice that comes too late)

Comhairle an drochchomhairligh.
Advice of the bad adviser.

Éist le comhairle an amadáin!
Listen to the advice of a fool!
(i.e. Even a fool can be right.)

An rud is annamh is iontach.
What is rare is wonderful.

Is maith an scáthán súil charad.
A friend's eye is a good mirror.

Moladh luath agus cáineadh mall.
Be quick to praise and slow to criticise.

Éist le fuaim na habhann agus gheobhaidh tú breac.
Listen to the sound of the river and you will catch a trout.

Is binn béal ina thost.
Sweet is the mouth that is silent.
(cf. Words are silver; silence is golden.)

Maireann croí éadrom i bhfad.
A light heart lives a long time.

Ní féidir dubh a chur ina gheal ach seal.
You can only make black white for a while.
(i.e. the truth will eventually come out)

Ní mar a shíltear a bhítear.
Things aren't always as you think they are.
(cf. Things aren't always as they seem.)

Níl neart go teacht le chéile.
There is no strength until we come together.
(i.e. strength in unity)

Is maith an scéalaí an aimsir.
Time is a good storyteller.
(cf. Time will tell.)

Tús maith leath na hoibre!
A good start is half the work.
(cf. Well begun is half done.)

An té nach gcuirfidh san earrach, ní bhainfidh san fhómhar.
He who does not sow in the spring shall not reap in the autumn.

Uireasa a mhéadaíonn cumha.
Absence makes the heart grow fonder.

Taithí a dhéanann máistreacht.
Practice brings mastery.
(cf. Practice makes perfect.)

Níor bhris focal maith fiacail riamh.
A good word never broke a tooth.
(cf. A kind word never hurt anyone.)

Ní fhanann tamall ná trá le haon duine.
Time and tide wait for no person.

Ná tabhair breith ar an gcéad scéal.
Don't make a judgement hearing only one story.
(i.e. Listen carefully to all sides of the argument before making a judgement.)

Is mairg don té gan chomhairle dea-mhná. Is mairg don té nach n-éisteann le comhairle dea-mhná.
It is woe to him who hasn't the advice of a good woman!

Ní thagann an óige faoi dhó.
Youth does not come twice.
(cf. Gather ye rosebuds while ye may.)

An té nach nglacann comhairle, glacfaidh sé comhrac.
He who does not take advice will take battle.

Ná déan mar a dhéanaim, déan mar a deirim.
Do as I say, not as I do.

13

Ní hé lá na gaoithe lá na scolb.
The windy day isn't the day for thatching.

Tús maith leath na hoibre!
A good start is half the work!

Is fearr rith maith ná drochsheasamh!
A good run is better than a bad stand.

Ballaí bána roimh thuras fada.
White walls before a long journey.
(i.e. Make sure everything is in order before you set off.)

Is fusa scaipeadh ná cruinniú.
Scattering is easier than gathering.

Ní mór don fhear beag bheith glic.
The little man must be cunning.

Is leor nod don eolach.
A hint is sufficient to the wise.
(i.e. Take a hint!)

Ní bhíonn meas ar an aonphort.
There is no respect for the single tune.
(cf. Variety is the spice of life.)

Buail an t-iarann te!
Strike while the iron is hot!

Ná mol agus ná cáin tú féin!
Don't praise and do not criticise yourself!

Ná glac pioc comhairle gan comhairle ban.
Never take advice without a woman's guidance.

Ná leathnaigh do bhratach mura bhfuil tú in ann í a chosaint.
Don't unfurl your flag unless you can defend it.

Lig dom lig duit.
Allow me, allow you.
(i.e. Live and let live.)

Is maith stró ach ní maith róstró.
Stress is good, but not too much stress.

Is fearr beagán cuidithe ná mórán trua!
A little help is better than a lot of pity!

Is fear lúbadh ná briseadh.
It is better to bend than to break.
(i.e. Be adaptable!)

An té a bhíonn amuigh fuaraíonn a chuid.
The food of the absent man goes cold.

Is fearrde dea-chomhairle ná pota óir.
Good advice is better than a pot of gold.

Éist le comhairle ó gach aon agus déan do chomhairle féin.
Listen to everyone's advice, but follow your own.

Le titim na hoíche briathra saoithe.
With nightfall come wise words.
(i.e. People get wise in their old age.)

Is calaoiseach comhairle caillí.
An old hag's advice is deceitful.

Draoi agus saoi an tiománaí ar chlaí.
The hurler on the sidelines is a druid and a wise man.

Ná mol d'fhear ar bith glacadh le scilling an Rí ná pósadh.
Do not advise any man to go to war or to marry.
(*'scilling an Rí'*—the King's shilling, was a soldier's payment for joining
the army and/or going to war.)

Ná téigh i muinín leighis atá níos measa ná an galar féin.
Avoid a cure that is worse than the disease.

Luath chun leapa agus luath éirí—mana an scafaire, saibhir is saoi.
Early to bed, early to rise, makes a man healthy, wealthy and wise.

Tagann caonach liath ar arán sa tigh, ach ar arán a roinntear bláth agus buí.
Mould grows on bread in the home, but bread that is shared brings prosperity and gratitude.
(cf. What we keep, we lose; what we give away we keep for ever.)

Ní féidir an ciseán ar fad a líonadh le húlla deasa.
The whole basket cannot be filled with nice apples.
(*Rabhadh Dánta*, Alan Titley, 1947—)

Ambition (*Uaillmhian*)

Is féidir le mac an diabhail bheith ina rí sa tír.
Even the son of the devil can be the king of the land.

Níl locht ar éirí go hard sa saol ach ar éirí in airde.
There's nothing wrong with getting on in the world, but don't become arrogant.

Ní ionann díocas agus cíocras.
Doing what it takes to achieve is not the same as craving something.

Uaillmhian abhógach nach léimeann sa diallait ach a thiteann ar an taobh eile.
Vaulting ambition, which o'erleaps itself, and falls on the other.'
(*Macbeth* (1, 7) William Shakespeare, 1564—1616)

Deireadh na huaillmhéine, tús an tsonais.
The end of ambition is the beginning of happiness.

Is ionann fear gan uaillmhian agus bean gan dealramh.
A man without ambition is like a woman without looks.

Anger (*Fearg*)

Coimhéad fearg fhear na foighne!
Beware the anger of the patient man!

Is deas an rud an beagán ach é a dhéanamh go maith.
Little is best if done well.

Múchadh feirge sofhreagra.
A gentle reply quenches anger.

Buile ghairid atá san fhearg.
Anger is short madness.

Múchann béile maith tine na feirge.
A good meal quenches the fire of anger.

Ní théann an fhearg agus an chiall i dtíos le chéile.
Good sense and anger do live in same house.

Deireadh na foighne buile.
The end of patience is rage.

Is fearr liom feargach ná fealltach.
I prefer anger rather than treachery/ deceit.
(i.e. It is better that a person express their anger rather than hiding it deceitfully.)

Animals (*Ainmhithe*)

Ní réiteoidh ainmhí allta choíche le hainmhí clóis.
A wild animal will never settle with a domesticated animal.

Ainmhí ait áilleacht.
Beauty is a strange beast.

Is measa bean gan fear maith ná beithíoch aingiallta.
A woman without a good man is worse than a mad beast.

Bíonn adharca fada ar na beithígh i gcéin.
There are long horns on the animals far away.
(cf. Faraway hills are green.)

Is fusa éalú ó bheithíoch buile ná ó mháthair do chéile.
It is easier to escape from a mad beast than from your mother-in-law.
(This is traditionally said by wives about interference from meddling mothers-in-law.)

Fear ocrach beithíoch mire sa teach.
A hungry man is a mad beast in the house.

Is minic a loit beithíoch allta beithíoch uasal.
A rough beast has often ruined a thoroughbred.

Birds (*Éin*)

Ag díol circe lá fliuch.
Selling a hen on a wet day.

Trom cearc i bhfad.
A hen is heavy over a long distance.
(i.e. Even small inconveniences can become heavy burdens over time.)

Léim choiligh ar charn aoiligh.
A cock's jump on a dung hill.
(i.e. One who brags about a worthless achievement.)

Ní sia gob an ghé ná gob an ghandail.
The goose's neck is no longer than the gander's.
(cf. What is sauce for the goose is sauce for the gander.)

Is leor don dreoilín a nead.
A wren has need only of its nest.

Is fearr éan i do dhorn ná péire ar an gcraobh.
A bird in your fist is worth a pair on a branch.
(cf. A bird in the hand is worth two in the bush.)

Aithnítear an t-éan de réir a chleití.
A bird is known by its feathers.

Ní athraíonn an t-éan a chleití sa doineann.
A bird does not change its feathers because the weather is bad.
(i.e. Even when times are difficult we shouldn't betray our principles.)

Cats (*Cait*)

Is é gnó an chait luch a mharú.
It is a cat's business to kill a mouse.

Cad a dhéanfaidh mac an chait ach luch a mharú?
What will the son of a cat do but kill a mouse?
(cf. Like father, like son.)

Nuair a bhíonn an cat amuigh bíonn na lucha ag rince.
When the cat is out, the mice are dancing.

Mac don chat an piscín.
The kitten is the son of the cat.
(cf. A chip off the old block/The apple doesn't fall far from the tree. i.e.
Children often inherit their parents' characteristics.)

Scéal an chait, a piscín.
The cat's life is its kitten.

Is aoibhinn leis an chat an t-iasc ach ní háil leis a chosa a fhliuchadh.
The cat likes the fish, but doesn't like to get its feet wet.
(i.e. Often said to a work-shy person who wishes to benefit from the
rewards of some other person's efforts.)

Ar mhaithe leis féin a dhéanann an cat crónán.
The cat purrs for its own benefit.

Tá cead ag an chat féachaint ar an rí.
The cat can look at the king.

Dhéanfadh sé cat agus dhá eireaball air.
He would make a cat with two tails.
(i.e. Don't believe a word he tells you.)

Beagán ar bheagán a d'ith an cat an scadán.
Bit by bit, the cat ate the herring.
(cf. *Ina dhiaidh a chéile a tógadh na caisleáin.*)

Bíonn gach cat liath san oíche.
Every cat looks grey at night.
(i.e. You have to have a clear view of what people do to know who they are.)

Bíonn dhá chat le luch aonair amhail beirt bhan agus teach léanmhar.
Two cats with one mouse is like two women in (charge of) one sorrowful house.
(i.e. You cannot have two women running the same house.)

Mura bhfuil cat sa teach beidh na lucha gan bhac.
If there isn't a cat in the house there'll be no stopping the mice.
(i.e. It's only reasonable to take sensible precautions.)

Cows (*Ba*)

Fear na haon bhó fear gan aon bhó.
A man with one cow is a man without a cow.
(i.e. The possession of one cow does not constitute wealth.)

Gach éinne ag cur a bhó féin thar abhainn.
Everyone puts their own cow over the river.
(i.e. Each person looks after their own interests.)

Rith na bó laige le fána.
The run of the weak cow downhill.
(i.e. The coward's way out.)

Géim bó i dtír namhad.
The bellowing of a cow in the land of the enemy.
(i.e. Keep quiet when you are surrounded by potentially hostile people.)

Troid na mbó maol.
A fight between bald cows.
(i.e. a harmless fight)

Bíonn gach duine lách go dtí go dtéann bó isteach ina gharraí féin.
Everyone is kind (and understanding) until a cow goes into their own garden.

Ba shaibhir fear na muice gur bhuail sé le fear na bó.
The man who owned the pig was rich till he met the man who owned a cow.
(i.e. wealth is relative)

23

Béarfaidh bó éigin gamhain éigin lá éigin.
Some cow will give birth to some calf some day.
(i.e. Something will eventually turn up.)

Is mór taibhseach adharca na mbó thar lear.
They are great and showy the horns of the cows abroad.
(cf. *Is glas iad na cnoic i bhfad uainn.*)

Don té a bhfuil samhlaíocht aige is bó seangán.
For him who has imagination, a cow is an ant or an ant is a cow.
(*Rabhadh Dánta*, Alan Titley, 1947—)

Gan bhó—gan stró!
No cows—no cares!
(i.e. If you have no responsibilities, you have no worries.)

Ní thógfadh Éire gamhain seanbhó.
The (whole of) Ireland couldn't raise the calf of an old cow.
(i.e. The children of older mothers are more difficult to raise because they're often spoilt. *An tOileánach,* Tomás Ó Criomhthain, 1856—1937.)

Dogs/Hounds (*Madraí/Cúnna/Gadhair*)

Is fearr madra beo ná leon marbh.
A live dog is better than a dead lion.

Nuair atá do lámh i mbéal an mhadra tarraing amach go bog é.
When your hand is in the dog's mouth, remove it gently.

Tabhair drochainm ar mhadra!
Give a dog a bad name!
(i.e. When a person gets a bad reputation it is hard to shake off.)

Is dána gach madra i ndoras a thí féin.
Every dog is brave in the doorway of its own house.

Is olc an cú nach fiú a liú.
It's a poor hound that isn't worth calling.

Coinnigh an chnámh is leanfaidh an madra thú.
Hold on to the bone and the dog will follow you.

Buail mo mhadra agus buail mé féin!
Hit my dog and (you) hit me.
(cf. Love me, love my dog!)

I gcosa con a bhíonn a cuid.
In the legs of the hound, her food is found.

An té a luíonn le madraí, éiríonn sé le dreancaidí.
He who lies with dog, rises with fleas.

Fish (*Iasc*)

Is fearr breac sa láimh ná bradán sa linn.
A trout in the hand is worth a salmon in the pool.

Éist le fuaim na habhann agus gheobhaidh tú breac.
Listen to the sound of a stream and you will catch a trout.

Tá breac san abhainn chomh maith is a gabhadh ann fós.
There is a trout in the river as good as any that has been caught.

Bíonn aoi cosúil le hiasc, tar éis trí lá bíonn boladh bréan uaidh.
A guest is like a fish: after three days it stinks.
(Italian proverb)

Más in iasc atá do dhúil, ná déan do shlí go Corrán Tuathail.
If you are interested in fish, don't make your way to Carrauntoohil.
(Carrauntoohil, at 1,038 metres, is the highest mountain in Ireland.)

Tabhair iasc do dhuine agus ní bheidh ocras air lá. Tabhair slat iascaigh dó,
beidh béile aige gach lá dá shaol.
Give a man a fish and he will not be hungry for a day. Give him a fishing
rod and he will eat a meal every day of his life.

Foxes (*Sionnaigh/Madraí Rua*)

Sionnach i gcraiceann na caorach.
A fox in a sheep's clothing.

Madra rua dhá uair ní mhealltar é.
The fox is not fooled twice.
(i.e. with the same trick)

Is saothrach an sealgaire ag súil le srianadh seansionnaigh le sás.
It's a busy hunter who tries to snare an old fox.
(i.e. The older people get, the harder it is to fool them.)

Ná bain an giorria ó bhéal an tsionnaigh agus beidh na cearca ó bhaol an tsionnaigh.
Do not snatch the hare from the fox's mouth and the hens will be safe from the fox.

Is cleasaí ciúin an sionnach ach is calma callánach an mac tíre.
The fox is a quiet trickster, but the wolf is brave and noisy.

Goats (*Gabhair*)

Cuir culaith shíoda ar ghabhar agus is gabhar is gcónaí é.
Put a silk suit on a goat, and it is still a goat.
(cf. You can't make a silk purse out of a sow's ear.)

Mura mbeadh agat ach gabhar bí i lár an aonaigh leis.
If you only have a goat, be in the middle of the fair with it.
(i.e. Don't hide your light under a bushel.)

Is fearr marcaíocht ar ghabhar ná coisíocht dá fheabhas.
It is better to ride on a goat than walking, however good it may be.

Olann a bhaint de ghabhar nó iarraidh abhrais ar phocán.
Seeking wool from a goat or yarn from a billy-goat.
(i.e. fruitless pursuits)

Má ligtear an gabhar isteach sa séipéal ní stopfaidh sé go haltóir.
If you let a goat into a chapel he won't stop until he reaches the altar.
(cf. Give him an inch and he'll take a mile.)

Hares and Rabbits
(*Giorraithe agus Coiníní*)

Más gasta an giorria, gabhtar é faoi dheireadh.
Even if the hare is fast, it is caught in the end.
(i.e. You can't escape fate, natural justice, life, etc.)

Tabhair lámh don obair agus póg do chois an ghiorria.
Shake hands with work and kiss the leg of the hare.
(i.e. live now and forget about the past, lost opportunities, etc.)

Is fearr greim de choinín ná dhá ghreim de chat.
One bite of a rabbit is better than two bites of a cat.
(i.e. Quality is better than quantity.)

Má ritheann tú i ndiaidh dhá choinín, ní bhfaighidh tú ceachtar díobh.
If you run after two rabbits, you will catch neither.
(Russian/Chinese proverb)

An coinín ag maslú cú marbh óna rapach féin.
The hare insulting the dead hound from its own burrow.

Dá rithfeá mar a thaoscann tú siar bhéarfá ar ghiorria nó ar leanaí Lir.
If you could run as you drink, you could catch a hare or the children of Lir.
(The children of Lir were bewitched by their evil stepmother who turned them into swans. They had to spend 300 years in Lough Derravaragh, 300 years on the Sea of Moyle, and 300 years on Inis Gluaire. They were eventually returned to their human form, and at last met St Patrick, who baptised them before they died.)

Hens (*Cearca*)

Is trom cearc i bhfad.
A hen is heavy if carried a long distance.

Is minic ubh mhór ag cearc bheag.
It is often a small hen lays a big egg.

Is olc an cearc nach scríobfaidh di féin.
It's a bad hen that will not scratch for itself.

Is maith an chearc nach mbeireann amuigh.
It is a good hen that doesn't lay its eggs outside.

Níor bhris cearc na sicíní a sprochaille riamh.
The hen with chickens never burst its craw.

Beireann cearc dhubh ubh bhán.
A black hen lays a white egg.

Horses (*Capaill*)

Capall na hoibre an bia.
The horse of work is food.
(i.e. The horse pulls the plough in the field or the cart to market, therefore without the horse the work cannot be done. It is the same with food: we must eat well to do our work well.)

Capall na beatha an grá.
The (work-)horse of life is love.
(cf. Love makes the world go round. This is obviously a play on '*Capall na hoibre an bia*'.)

Is minic a rinne bromach gioblach capall cumasach.
It is often that a ragged colt made a powerful horse.

Ní dhéanfadh an saol capall rása d'asal.
Life will not make a racehorse out of a donkey.

Mair a chapaill agus gheobhaidh tú féar!
Live horse and you will get grass!
(i.e. telling people who are dying of starvation that all they have to do is to live and eventually they will get food)

Tosach staile nó deireadh lárach!
The front of a stallion, the rear of a mare!
(i.e. Stand clear of these locations!)

Do spoir féin ach capall duine eile.
Your own spurs, but someone else's horse.
(i.e. Don't abuse property borrowed from others.)

Scéal do chapall ina chodladh é.
A story being told to a horse that's asleep.
(i.e. The listener has no interest in the story being told.)

Ag lorg a chapaill agus gan fios a dhatha aige.
Looking for his horse not knowing what colour it is.
(i.e. involved in a task without the necessary understanding to succeed)

Capall a chur mar a dtreabhann sé.
To set a horse (to work) by what it ploughs.
(i.e. to give a person work according to their ability)

Srathair na hainnise ar chapall na tubaiste.
The yoke of misfortune upon the horse of calamity.
(i.e. If it isn't one thing, it's another!)

Is capall gabhar más gá.
The goat is a horse if necessary.
(i.e. In difficult times we must use what is available.)

Capall an tsaoil an t-airgead.
The horse of life is money.
(i.e. Money makes the world go round.)

Insects (*Feithidí*)

Aithníonn ciaróg ciaróg eile.
One beetle recognises another.
(cf. Birds of a feather flock together.)

Gach damhán alla ag tochras ar a cheirtlín féin.
Every spider spinning its own web.
(i.e. Everyone looking after their own interests.)

Don té a bhfuil samhlaíocht aige is bó seangán.
For him who has imagination, a cow is an ant or an ant is a cow.
(*Rabhadh Dánta*, Alan Titley, 1947—)

Sa chogadh idir eilifint agus seangáin; maraíonn an eilifint na mílte le gach coiscéim ach sa deireadh beidh an bua ag na seangáin.
In a war between an elephant and ants, each step the elephant takes kills a thousand ants, but in the end the ants win.
(Attributed to a German General on the Eastern Front during World War Two.)

Mice (*Lucha*)

An rud nach bhfuil agus nach mbeidh, nead ag an luch i bhféasóg an chait.
What isn't and will never be—a mouse's nest in a cat's beard.

'Nuair a thagann an ceann cait go picnic na luch, ní hé chun páirt a ghlacadh sna sacrásaí.'
'When an owl comes to a mouse picnic, it's not there to take part in the sack races' (Tomasz Banacek).
(i.e. When, for example, a beautiful young woman takes an interest in an old man, she most likely has some ulterior motive!)

I súile na luiche is leon cat.
In the eyes of the mouse, a cat is a lion.

Lá spóirt ag an gcat—lá báis don luch.
A day of fun for the cat—a day of death for the mouse.

Is cróga an luch a dhéanann a nead i gcluas cait.
It's a brave mouse that nestles in a cat's ear.

Pigs (*Muca*)

Radharc na muice lá gaoithe.
A pig's sight on a windy day.
(i.e. unfathomable ability, whatever is unexplainable but true)

Nár chaithe an mhuc a laincis.
May the pig not wear its fetter.
(i.e. of the unworthiness a person to wear such elegant clothes. cf. Mutton dressed as lamb.)

Tá éisteacht na muice bradaí aige.
He has the thieving pig's ability to hear.
(i.e. He misses nothing; he can overhear even a whisper.)

Ag cuimilt blonaige de thóin na muice méithe.
Rubbing lard into the backside of the fat pig.
(i.e. (i) laying it on thick; overdoing it; (ii) riding the gravy-train)

Na muca ciúine a itheann an mhin.
The silent pigs eat the meal.
(i.e. It's the quiet ones who get things done.)

Sheep/Lambs (*Caoirigh agus Uain*)

Ná díol caora dhubh, ná cheannaigh caora dhubh, agus ná bí gan chaora dhubh.
Don't sell a black sheep, don't buy a black sheep, and don't be without a black sheep.

Caora mhór an t-uan i bhfad.
It's a large sheep, the lamb over a long distance.
(i.e. Even small inconveniences can become heavy burdens over time.)

Is minic a bhí uan bán ag caora dhubh.
It is often that a black sheep has a white lamb.
(i.e. Good can come from evil.)

Ní tréad caora.
One sheep is not a flock.

Is minic a cailleadh caora mhaith i ngeall ar luach leathphingine de tharra.
It is often a sheep is lost for a halfpenny's worth of tar.
(i.e. Beware of false economies.)

Anticipation (*Tnúth*)

Is minic gur fearr tnúth na mara ná trú na mara.
Longing to go to sea is often better than being a wretch out at sea.
(The word '*tnúth*' is pronounced '*trú*' in Donegal Irish, so this is a play on two words spelled differently but sounding the same.)

Cuir an breac san eangach sula gcuire tú sa phota é!
Get the fish into the net before you put it in the pot!

Ní breac é go bhfuil sé ar an bport.
It isn't a fish until you've landed it.

Ná déan cró roimh airc.
Don't make a pigsty before the piglets have arrived.

Is fál ar an ngort é i ndiaidh na foghla.
It is no good closing the stable door after the horse has bolted.

Cothaíonn feitheamh fonn.
Waiting (for something) makes it more exciting.

Appearance (*Dealramh*)

Ní mar a shíltear an bhítear.
Things aren't always as they seem.

Ní ionann i gcónaí cófra agus a lucht.
A cupboard does not speak of its contents.
(i.e. Appearances can be deceptive.)

Is minic a bhí dealraitheach cailliúnach.
It is often that what looks good fails to live up to expectations.

Buailtear le daoine ar ghalántacht a gcallaí,
Ach in éirim a gcinn atá breáthacht an bhealaigh.
We meet people because of their elegant clothes,
But we accompany them because of their intellect/wit.

Dhá dtrian den bhua—dealramh.
Two thirds of victory is appearance.

Is minic a bhíonn an t-úll dearg go holc ina chroí.
It is often that a red apple has a bad core.

Appetite (*Goile*)

Is maith an t-anlann an t-ocras.
Hunger is the best sauce.

Is maith an mustard an sliabh.
The mountain is a good mustard.
(i.e. Climbing a mountain can create a good appetite.)

Tagann an goile le hitheachán.
Appetite comes with eating.

An té gan goile don chath beidh sé gan uile go bráth.
He who has no appetite for battle will always have nothing.

An té gan goile don chéachta macánta, bíodh goile aige don dréacht diaganta.
The one who has no appetite for the honest plough, let him have an appetite for the holy scripture.
(i.e. It's either work or the priesthood.)

Marbh le tae agus marbh gan é.
Dead from the tea and dead without it.
(i.e. You can have too much or too little of anything.)

Is fearr bheith ar lorg bia ná goile.
It is better to be looking for food than an appetite.

Application (*Cur chuige*)

Ní fhaigheann cos ina cónaí aon ní.
A stick-in-the-mud gets nothing.

Leath na ceirde an uirlis.
Half the work is (having the right) tool.

Ní fhaightear saill gan saothar.
Fat is not got without toil.

Is trian den obair tús a chur.
A third of the work is to make a start.

Is fearr éirí go moch ná suí go mall.
It is better to get up early than to stay up late.

Trom an t-ualach an leisce.
Laziness is a heavy burden.

Cuir luath agus bain luath.
Sow early and reap early.

As obair a fhaightear an fhoghlaim.
From work learning is acquired.

Gnáthamh na hoibre an t-eolas.
The practice of work brings knowledge.

Asking (*Iarraidh*)

Iarraigí agus gheobhaidh sibh.
Ask and ye shall receive.
(Biblical)

Ní peaca guí a iarraidh.
It's not a sin to ask.

Is fearr slí a iarraidh ná dul ar iarraidh.
It's better to ask the way than to go astray.

Faigheann iarraidh iarraidh eile.
(i) Seeking for one thing will find another.
(ii) Request for request is all fair. (i.e. If someone asks a favour of you, then you are entitled to request one in return.)

Diúltú tréan don achainí atá faon.
A limp request invites a firm refusal.

Iarraigí agus tabharfar daoibh.
Ask and ye shall receive.
(Biblical)

Authority (*Údarás*)

Is fearr i gceannas ná sa cheann.
It is better to rule than to be oppressed.

Tagann údarás le haois.
Authority comes with age.

Má tá achainí agat ar an rí, labhair ar dtús le bean an tí.
If you have a request of the king, first speak to the woman of the house.
(On the islands, a 'king' was chosen by the islanders to be their representative and leader. This proverb suggests that the king's wife was usually a person of considerable influence and authority in the village. In a more general sense it also suggests that even the most powerful men are in fact 'under the thumb' of their wives!)

Scéal gan údar—scéal gan údarás.
A story without an author is a story without authority.

Réimeas gan réimse ainriail.
Power without limit is tyranny.

Beauty (*Áilleacht*)

Nochtann grá gnaoi.
Beauty is in the eye of the beholder.

Is minic a bhí gránna greannmhar agus daoi dathúil.
It is often that ugly was fun and handsome was glum.

Is minic a bhíonn breá bréan.
It is often that beauty is foul.

Ná togh bean gan máchail.
Do not choose a woman (for marriage) without blemish.

Ná togh bean ar a scéimh.
Do not choose a woman (for marriage) by her beauty.

Ní hí an áilleacht a chuireann an corcán ag fiuchadh.
Beauty does not make the pot boil.

Begging (*An Déirc*)

Is buí le bocht an beagán.
Beggars can't be choosers.

Ná bac le mac an bhacaigh agus ní bhacfaidh mac an bhacaigh leat.
Don't bother the beggar's son, and the beggar's son won't bother you.

Déan taise le déirceach is déanfaidh Dia taise leat.
Have pity on the beggar, and God will have pity on you.

Tagann na haingil i riocht lucht déircigh.
Angels appear in the form of beggars.

Ní fhaigheann síor-iarraidh ach síor-eiteach.
Constant begging only meets with constant refusal.

Déirc dá chuid féin a thabhairt d'amadán.
To give a fool alms from what is his.
(cf. to feed a dog its own tail)

Is cuma leis an bhacach cé a líonann a mhála.
The beggar doesn't mind who fills his bag.
(i.e. Giving alms on Sunday is our due and is of little value.)

Is fearr pocán i do lámh ná pollán i do bholg.
It's better to have a begging bag in your hand than a hollow space in your belly.

Is breá le Dia lucht tugtha déirce.
God loves alms-givers.

Tá geataí ifrinn dúnta go deo ar chroí oscailte.
The gates of hell are always closed to an open heart.

Flaitheas Dé don té nár shéan an déirceach.
The realms of God for him who did not deny the beggar.
(i.e. In Irish tradition all beggars are mystical or even divine figures.
Often they are seen as angels in disguise, or beings with supernatural
powers. Therefore, beggars were treated with great respect.)

Dá bhfíoródh gach guí, bheadh bacach ina rí.
If every wish came true, the beggar would be king.

Óige caite le baois, déirc á lorg le haois.
A youth wasted foolishly will mean begging in old age.

Ní bhíonn déirceach eaglach roimh ghadaí.
A beggar does not fear the thief.

Beginning (*Tús/Tosach*)

Tús/Tosach maith leath na hoibre.
A good start is half the work.

Chun obair mhór a chríochnú, ní mór tús beag a chur leis.
To finish great work, it must have a small beginning.

Tosaíonn gach bliain leis an gcéad lá.
Every year starts with the first day.

Tosach sláinte codladh.
The beginning of recovery is sleep.

Bíonn gach tús lag.
Every beginning is weak.

An turas is faide sa saol tosaíonn sé le coiscéirn amháin.
The longest journey in life starts with one small step.

Belief (*Creideamh*)

Déanann feiceáil fírinne.
Seeing is believing.

Cláraíonn creideamh cnoc.
Faith flattens mountains.

Creideamh ag an tuath, eolas ag an tsaoi.
The unlearned person has faith; the learned knows.

Is é an t-amhras eochair na tuisceana.
Doubt is the key to understanding.

Mura bhfuil creideamh i do chroí ní féidir aon ní.
Without faith, you can do nothing.

Bogann creideamh sléibhte.
Faith can move mountains.
(English proverb)

Blessings (*Beannachtaí*)

Go méadaí Dia do stór!
May God increase your store!

Go raibh gach ní dá bhreáthacht agat!
May you have the best of everything!

Go dtuga Dia ciall duit!
May God give you sense!

Go raibh an rath ag rith ort!
May you always be lucky!

Go saolaí Dia thú!
May God grant you long life!

Go bhfága Dia do shláinte agat!
May God leave good health with you!

(Go raibh) sliocht sleachta ar shliocht bhur sleachta!
The progeny of your progeny upon the progeny of your progeny!
(i.e. May your children have children, and their children have children!)

Go dté tú slán!
May you have a safe journey!

Go n-éirí an bóthar leat!
The best of luck on your trip! Bon voyage!

Go dtagair slán!
May you arrive safely!

Go luaithí Dia duit!
God speed!

Go saora Dia ón urchóid sinn!
May God deliver us from harm!

Go rabhair slán!
May you be safe!

Go gcrosa Dia sin!
May God prevent that!

Go n-éiste Dia leat!
May God listen to you!
(i.e. hear your prayer)

Dia go deo leat!
(May) God always be with you!

Go mbeannaí Dia thú!
May God bless you!

Go mbeirimid beo ar an am seo arís!
May we (all) be alive at this time next year!

Go raibh Nollaig shona agus athbhliain faoi mhaise duit!
May you have a merry Christmas and a happy New Year!

Gurab amhlaidh duit!
The same to you!

Nár laga Dia do lámh!
May God not weaken your hand!
(i.e. thanking someone for a kindness)

Nár bhuaile crá ná ciapadh thú!
May you not be tormented or afflicted!

Nár rabhair riamh gan chúnamh!
May you never be without help!

Ná raibh godamat ort!
May you never be in squalor!
(cf. *500 Beannacht le Breandán Mac Gearailt, lch. 26.*)
('*godamat*'—dirt)

Nár thé tú ar strae choíche!
May you never lose your way!

Nár phósair go brách arís!
May you never wed again!
(i.e. May both of you live long lives in wedded bliss.)

Ná raibh grinneall id ghrá-sa!
May your love never have an end!
('*grinneall*' is the abyss or the 'bed' of a lake, sea, etc.)

Nár dhaora Dia thú!
May God not condemn you!

Nár chrá Dia choíche thú!
May God never torment you!

Blindness (*Daille*)

An dall ag giollaíocht an daill.
The blind leading the blind.

Aimsíonn an dall a bhéal.
The blind man can find his mouth.

I ríocht na ndall is rí fear na leathshúile.
In the kingdom of the blind, the one-eyed man is king.

Ceileann súil an rud atá léir don dall féin.
The eye conceals the thing that even the blind person can see.

Níl aon dall chomh dall leis an té nach dteastaíonn uaidh a shúile a oscailt.
There are none so blind as those who do not wish to see.

Boats (*Báid*)

Is maith an bád a dhéanann amach an caladh a d'fhág sé.
It is a good boat that finds the harbour it left.

Éiríonn na báid le hairde na taoide.
The boat rises with the tide.
(i.e. All things depend on one another.)

Téann na longa móra thar sáile ach fanann na baidíní cois cuain sa bhaile.
The great ships go overseas, but the little boats stay near the bay at home.

Bristear long le linn an ghála, t'r éis mórála lucht a tógála.
The ship is lost in the gale after much boasting by its builders.

Is ionann an t-uisce ar an dá thaobh den bhád.
The water is the same on both sides of the boat.

Ná corraigh an bád!
Don't rock the boat!
(English proverb)

Body (*Corp*)

Ní sochraid go corp!
There isn't a funeral until there's a corpse.
(i.e. said to someone who has another person buried before there is any definite news of his/her death, e.g. a woman waiting for a son or a husband to return home from sea)

Is ionann corp gan ceann agus ceann gan toil.
Being unfree is the same as having a body without a head.
('*ceann gan toil*—being prohibited from doing what you want to do)

Cónaíonn anam folláin i gcorp sláintiúil.
A healthy soul lives in a healthy body.

Go parthas Dé anam an duine, a chorp cré chun na gcruimheanna agus a stór saoil dá lucht gaoil.
The person's soul goes to paradise, his earthly body to the worms, and (all) his worldly goods to his relatives.

Ear (*Cluas*)

Cá raibh tusa aimsir na gcluas?
Where were you at the time of ears?
(i.e. to someone who is not listening, referring to the possibility that the person was absent when God was handing out the gift of hearing)

Bíonn cluasa ar an claíocha.
There are ears on the ditches.
(cf. The walls have ears.)

An rud nach gcloiseann an chluas ní chuireann sé buairt ar an gcroí.
What is not heard by the ear does not upset the heart.

Dhéanfadh sé nead i do chluas.
He would make a nest in your ear.
(i.e. about a person who is not to be trusted, a con-artist or smooth-talking trickster)

Eye (*Súil*)

Feiceann súil ghruama saol gruama.
A gloomy eye sees a gloomy life.

Is fearr súil sa chúinne ná dhá shúil ar fud an tí.
An eye in the corner is worth two eyes all round the house.

Is fearr súil romhat ná dhá shúil i do dhiaidh.
One eye in front of you is better than two eyes behind you.

Seachnaíonn an tsúil an rud nach bhfeiceann.
The eye avoids the thing it cannot see.
(i.e. out of sight, out of mind)

Is dall súil i gcúil duine eile.
It is blind the eye in another person's abode.
(i.e. We don't know where anything is in another person's abode.)

I ríocht na ndall is rí fear aonroisc.
In the kingdom of the blind, the one-eyed man is king.

Bíonn súil le muir ach ní bhíonn súil le huaigh.
There is an eye (i.e. hope) for the sea, but none for the grave.

Hand (*Lámh*)

Is beag rud nach faide ná do lámh.
It's the rare thing that is not longer than your hand.
(i.e. Any instrument is better than working with one's bare hands.)

Ná bíodh do lámh i mbéal an mhadra.
Don't have your hand in the dog's mouth.
(i.e. Don't look for trouble.)

Is minic gur fearr lámh ladrainn ná lámh eadrainn.
The hand of the robber (i.e. death) can often be better than the hand of marriage.

Is fearr bheith faoi loime láimhe ná (faoi) throime láimhe.
It is better to be bare of hand than under a cruel hand.
(i.e. Poverty is better than cruelty.)

Is bocht an lámh gan mámh ná dáimh!
It is a poor hand without a trump card or fellow-feeling.
(i.e. said by one who, out of kindness, is assisting another by cunning)

Head (*Ceann*)

Is fearr maol ná bheith gan ceann.
It's better to have no hair than to have no head.

An té nach bhfuil ceann láidir air ní mór dó cosa láidre a bheith faoi.
He who hasn't a good head must have strong legs.
(i.e. If you have a poor memory, or are scatterbrained, you will have to do a lot more walking.)

Chuirfeadh sé cosa chrainn faoi na cearca.
He would put wooden legs under the hens.
(cf. He'd promise you the sun, moon and stars. i.e. Don't believe him!)

Is ón cheann a thagann an cheird.
The craft comes from the head.

Is ionann corp gan ceann agus ceann gan toil.
A headless body is the same as being unfree.
('*ceann gan toil*—being prohibited from doing what you want to do)

Ní féidir ceann críonna a chur ar ghualainn óig.
It is not possible to put a wise head on a young shoulder..

Heart (*Croí*)

Maireann croí éadrom i bhfad.
A light heart lives longest.

Ní bhíonn aon duine aosta ina chroí.
No person is old in their heart.
(i.e. Even though their body grows old, people do not age in their soul.)

Is fearr teolaí croí ná eolaí daoi.
A warm, kind heart is better than boorish, learned man.

Is fusa aghaidh duine a aithint ná a chroí.
It is easier to know a man's face than his heart.

An croí atá i ngrá leis an saol, dósan atá sonas thar maoil.
The heart that loves life will have happiness to overflowing.

Uireasa a mhéadaíonn cumha croí.
Absence makes the heart grow fonder.

Is feasach don chroí rudaí nach dtuigeann réasún ar bith.
The heart has its reasons of which reason knows nothing.
(Blaise Pascal, 1623—1662)

Feet/Legs (*Cosa*)

Ní fhaigheann cos ina cónaí dada.
A stay-at-home/stick-in-the-mud achieves nothing.

An té a bhíonn thíos buailtear cos air.
The one who is down is walked over.

Bíonn leathchos ar an fhírinne ach dhá chos ar an mbréag.
A lie has two feet but the truth is lame.

Bíonn cosa crua faoi chapall na comharsan.
The neighbour's horse has strong legs.
(i.e. referring to the mistreatment of something borrowed, or disrespect
for another's property. One takes better care of one's own horse than one's
neighbour's horse.)

Tá cos leis san uaigh agus cos eile ar a bruach.
He has one foot in the grave and another on its edge.
(cf. *Tá sé ag comhrá leis an mbás.*)

Mouth (*Béal*)

Is binn béal ina thost.
A silent mouth is sweet.

Is minic a bhris béal duine a shrón.
It's often a man's mouth broke his nose.

Deartháir don bhréag an béal bán.
Flattery is akin to lying.

An rún i gcroí an fhir chiallmhair atá ar bhéal an mheisceora.
The secret in the heart of the sober man is on the lips of the drunkard.
(lit. in the mouth of the drunkard.)

Ní théann cuileoga isteach i mbéal druidte.
A closed mouth catches no flies.
(Miguel de Cervantes, 1547—1616)

Meon múinte, lámh cúnta agus béal dúnta.
An educated manner, a helping hand and a closed mouth.

As a béal a chrúitear an bhó.
Because of its mouth (i.e. of what it eats), the cow is milked.
(cf. An army marches on its stomach.)

Stomach/Belly (*Bolg*)

Ní líontar an bolg le caint.
Talk does not fill the belly.

Bolg gan greim bia, ceann gan ciall mhór.
There's not much sensible thinking on an empty stomach.

Ná díol d'anam ar do bholg!
Do not sell your soul for your belly!
(cf. Do not sell your soul for a mess of pottage.)

Ní dhéantar siúl fada ar bholg folamh!
A long walk is not made on an empty stomach!
(i.e. an invitation to someone who is about to leave on a long journey to join you in a meal)

Ná bíodh do bhéal níos mó ná do bholg!
Don't let your eyes be bigger than your belly!
(cf. Don't bite off more than you can chew!)

Bolgam tae i mbolg an lae!
(It's good to take) a sip of tea in the middle of the day.
(i.e. an invitation to take a break)

Throat (*Scornach*)

An gad is giorra don scornach is gá a réiteach ar dtús.
The knot nearest the throat should be dealt with first.
(i.e. The most pressing problem should be resolved first.)

Ná gearradh do theanga do scornach.
Don't let your tongue cut your throat.

Greim sceadamáin ar an mbeatha is ea an fhilíocht.
Poetry is a way of taking life by the throat.
(Robert Frost, 1874—1963)

Nuair atá an bás i ngreim scrogaill ort, is cuma faoin deismireacht chainte.
When death grabs you by the throat, polite speech doesn't matter.
(i.e. All the niceties of social intercourse dissipate in a time of crisis.)

*Dhá imní mná—báid gan filleadh ón mhuir agus glothar an bháis i
scornach a fir.*
Two matters of concern for a woman—boats that don't return from the
sea and the death-rattle in the throat of her husband.
(see also: Triads)

Tongue (*Teanga*)

Is éasca gach uile rud a dhéanamh ar do theanga.
It is easy to do everything with your tongue.
(cf. Talk is cheap.)

Teanga fhada ach cos ghairid.
A long tongue but a short leg.
(cf. long on talk, short on action)

Tabharfaidh do theanga chun na Róimhe thú.
Your tongue will bring you to Rome.
(i.e. The gift of the gab will get you a long way in the world.)

Is minic a ghearr duine a scornach lena theanga féin.
It is often that person cut his throat with his own tongue.

Tá dhá chluas ort agus teanga amháin – mar sin bí ag éisteacht an dá oiread níos mó ná mar a labhraíonn tú.
You have two ears and one tongue, therefore listen twice as much as you speak.

Bogann an fíon an teanga.
Wine loosens the tongue.

Borrowing (*Iasachtaí*)

Ná bíodh fiacha fear ort agus ná bíodh fiacha fear agat.
Do not owe debts to men, and do not have men owe you debts.
(cf. Neither a borrower nor a lender be.)

Agatsa cuid nach leat ach ar feadh tamaill, agus do chuid féin imithe uait go deo.
You have what is not yours for only a while, and what is yours you must give away forever.
(i.e. If you borrow money, for example, you have it for only a while: ultimately it has to be returned to the lender.)

Capall ar iasacht, capall gan aird.
A borrowed horse is an uncared for horse.

Is fearr ceannacht ná iasacht.
It is better to buy than to borrow.

Breeding (*Tógáil/Pórú*)

An rud a bheirtear sa chnámh, is doiligh a bhaint as an bhfeoil.
A thing that is in the bone is difficult to remove from the flesh.
(i.e. Breeding shows.)

Is treise dúchas ná oiliúint.
Nature is stronger than nurture.

Is bodmhadra gan mhaith a thabharfadh bata chun soithe.
It is a worthless dog without breeding that would strike a bitch with a stick.
(i.e. No man should lift a hand against his wife or any woman.)

Ní bheirtear bean, déantar í.
A woman is not born a woman, she becomes one.
(cf. '*On ne naît pas femme: on le devient.*' Simone de Beauvoir,
1908—1986)

Bíonn dealramh galánta ar chapall rása fiú gan diallait ghreanta air.
A racehorse looks elegant even without a polished/shapely saddle.
(i.e. Good breeding and upbringing do not require fine attire to be noticed.)

Brevity (*Gontacht*)

Beagán a rá agus a rá go maith.
Say little and say it well.

Más gearr é do scéal is greannmhar.
If your story is shorter, it is funnier.

Ní théann scéal grinn chun leadráin.
Brevity is the soul of wit.
(*Hamlet* (4,5). William Shakespeare, 1564—1616)

An rud is giorra is géire.
The shorter, the sharper.
(i.e. Keep it short and snappy.)

Bí dáiríre, bí go gairid agus bí i do shuí!
Be sincere, be brief and be seated!
(Franklin D. Roosevelt, 1882—1945)

Mura féidir leat rud a rá i gcúpla focal, úsáid focal amháin.
If you cannot say something in a couple of words, use one word.

Bribery (*Breabaireacht*)

Scoilteann breab cloch.
A bribe breaks a stone.

Ní háil le Dia lucht na breibe.
God doesn't like people who indulge in bribery.

An rud nach féidir le Bíobla, is féidir le breab.
What cannot be achieved by honest means can be achieved by bribery.

Is ionann breab agus maslú Dé.
A bribe is the same as insulting God.

An áit a bhfuil ganntanais saoil, bíonn na breabanna ag cur thar maoil.
Wherever there are shortages in life, there you will find bribery in abundance.

Bladar, breabaireacht agus biotáille—an triúr diabhal sa tír.
The three devils in the country are empty talk, bribery and drink.

Tarraing ar na maidí, tarraing chú't do bhean,
'S ná glac aon rud le do shaol le crúibín cam.
Pull on the oars, hug close to your wife,
And never take backhanders ever in your life.
(*'glacadh le crúibín cam'*—the taking of backhanders)

Church (*An Eaglais*)

Má tá ceart ag Dia, tá an dá cheart ag an Eaglais.
If God is right, the Church is twice as right.

Éisteann an Eaglais lena gcloiseann an sagart.
The Church listens to what the priest hears (but perhaps the priest doesn't always hear too well).

Má tá an sagart balbh tá a thréad dealbh.
If the priest is dumb then his flock are in poverty.

Ní fhaigheann sagart balbh beatha.
A dumb priest doesn't get a living.
(i.e. If you want to get on, you have got to speak up and be heard.)

Sagart maith baile faoi bhláth (sagart gan mhaith baile gan rath).
A good priest and the town blossoms (a useless priest and the town flounders).
(i.e. Much depended on the priest as to the relationship between the tenants and their English landlords.)

Ná bí beag agus ná bí mór leis an gcléir.
Neither be too unfriendly nor too friendly with the clergy.

Cleanness (*Glaine*)

Is den ghlóire an ghlaine.
Cleanliness belongs to what is glorious.
(cf. Cleanliness is next to Godliness.)

Is cuid den obair salachar.
Part of the work is getting dirty.

Téann an salachar lámh le láimh le saibhreas.
Dirt walks hand in hand with wealth.
(i.e. You won't get wealthy if you're afraid to get your hands dirty.)

Duine glan—duine slán!
A clean person is a healthy person.

Leath den tsláinte an ghlaine.
Half of health is being clean.

Bíonn an tsláintíocht níos tábhachtaí ná an neamhspleáchas polaitiúil.
Sanitation is more important than political independence.
(Mahatma Gandhi, 1869—1948)

Cleverness (*Clisteacht*)

Ní mór don fhear beag bheith glic.
The small man needs to be cunning.

Is treise cloigeann cliste ná maide smíste.
A smart head is stronger than a cudgel.

An rud is miste is féidir go cliste.
The thing that is not allowed can be achieved by cleverness.

Tagann an chlisteacht le cleachtadh an tsaoil.
Cleverness/know-how comes with experience.

Is den chlisteacht an tost.
Silence is part of being clever.

Is faide d'fhéasóg ná d'éirim mar a dúirt an sionnach leis an ngabhar.
More beard than brains, as the fox said to the goat.
(i.e. The external attributes do not reflect the substance.)

Clothes and Shoes
(*Éadaí agus Bróga*)

Is é an duine an t-éadach.
Clothes are the person.
(cf. Clothes maketh the man.)

Ní faisean go draoibeal!
There's no fashion until mud.
(The Seabhac says that this refers to women wearing dresses that were so long they were dragged in the mud. It can be used for any kind of ridiculous or quirky fashion.)

Ní hualach do dhuine a bhrat ná a bhróga.
It is no burden to a person their cloak or their shoes.
(i.e. What is essential to living is never a burden.)

An té ar cúng leis a bhróg is beag leis an saol.
A person whose shoe doesn't fit despises the world.

Mac an ghréasaí gan bhróga.
The son of the cobbler without shoes.

Seanbhróg smeartha bróg nua.
A polished old shoe is a new shoe.

Ní bhíonn a fhios ag duine cá luíonn an bhróg ar dhuine eile.
No one knows where the shoe pinches the other person.

Is cuma le fear na mbróg cá gcuireann sé a chos.
The man who wears shoes doesn't mind where he puts his feet.
(i.e. Those without need to be more careful for they have less protection.
This proverb was once rather dubiously used in a campaign for safer sex.)

Is mór an mhaise ar sheanbhróg búcla.
A buckle is a fine adornment on an old shoe.
(i.e. Even older people can benefit from wearing something pretty.)

Is giorra do dhuine a léine ná a chóta.
A person's shirt is closer than their coat.
(cf. Charity begins at home/Blood is thicker than water.)

Dá ghile an t-éadach is ea is fusa é a shalú.
The brighter the cloth the easier it is to dirty.

Osclaíonn callaí cuí bealaí agus hallaí rí.
Fine and appropriate clothing opens passageways and regal halls.
(cf. Good clothes open all doors.)

Suim mná óige san fhear agus ina bhróga.
A young woman's interest is in the man and the shoes he's wearing.
(i.e. A woman pays a lot of attention to the shoes of any man she fancies
because they might indicate social status.)

Comparisons (*Comparáidí*)

Aibí *chomh haibí le spideog.*
as fresh as a robin

Aosta *chomh haosta leis an gceo.*
as old as the mist

Ard *chomh hard leis an spéir.*
as high as the sky

Balbh *chomh balbh le cloch.*
as dumb/mute as a stone

Bán *chomh bán leis an sneachta.*
as white as the snow

Beag *chomh beag le luch fhéir.*
as small as field-mouse

Baoth *chomh baoth le lao na bó.*
as foolish as a cow's calf

Beo *chomh beo le cat.*
as lively as a cat

Binn *chomh binn leis an smólach.*
as sweet (sounding) as the thrush

Bocht *chomh bocht le bairneach.*
as poor as a limpet

Bodhar *chomh bodhar le slis.*
as deaf as a doorpost

Bog *chomh bog le him.*
as soft as butter

Bréagach *chomh bréagach le moladh meisceora.*
as false as a drunkard's praise

Bréan *chomh bréan le pluais an mhadra rua.*
as foul-smelling as the den of a fox

Buí *chomh buí le hór.*
as yellow as gold

Caite *chomh caite le seanbhróg.*
as worn as an old shoe

Cam *chomh cam le hadharc reithe.*
as crooked as a ram's horn

Caoch *chomh caoch le bonn bhróige.*
as blind as the sole of my shoe

Caol *chomh caol le cú.*
as thin as a hound

Casta *chomh casta le hadharc gabhair.*
as twisted/complicated as a goat's horn

Ceanndána *chomh ceanndána le muc.*
as obstinate as a pig

Ceart *chomh ceart is tá ceart ann.*
as right as right can be

Ciallmhar *chomh ciallmhar le Sola.*
as sensible as Solomon

Cinnte *chomh cinnte is tánn tú beo.*
as sure as you're alive

Ciúin *chomh ciúin leis an uaigh.*
as silent as the grave

Corrthónach *chomh corrthónach le cearc ar ghrideall te.*
as fidgety as a hen on a hot griddle

Cothrom *chomh cothrom le clár.*
as flat as a plank

Cráite *chomh cráite le scadán.*
as tormented as a herring

Crua *chomh crua le cloch.*
as hard as a stone

Crosta *chomh crosta le cat crainn.*
as irritable as a cat in a tree

Daingean *chomh daingean le carraig.*
as steady as a rock

Dall *chomh dall le smután.*
as blind as a stump

Dána *chomh dána le muc.*
as bold as a pig

Daor *chomh daor leis an donas.*
as dear/expensive as ill-luck

Díomhaoin *chomh díomhaoin le lúidín an phíobaire.*
as idle as a piper's little finger

Discréideach *chomh discréideach le bosca na faoistine.*
as discreet/secretive as the confessional

Domhain *chomh domhain leis an fharraige.*
as deep as the sea

Dorcha *chomh dorcha le pic.*
as dark as pitch

Dubh *chomh dubh le gual.*
as black as coal

Dúr *chomh dúr le seanasal.*
as dour/obstinate as an old donkey

Éadrom *chomh héadrom le cleite/le sop.*
as light as a feather/as a straw

Éaganta *chomh héaganta le cearc.*
as flighty/silly/hare-brained as a hen

Éasca *chomh héasca lena bhfaca tú riamh.*
as easy as you have ever seen

Fada *chomh fada leis an lá amárach.*
as long as the tomorrow

    chomh fada siar is atá siar ann.
    as far back as back goes

Falsa *chomh falsa le maide lofa.*
as lazy as a rotten stick

Fíor *chomh fíor leis an ngréin.*
as true as the sun

Fliuch *chomh fliuch leis an fharraige.*
as wet as the sea

Folláin *chomh folláin le breac.*
as healthy as a trout

Foighneach *chomh foighneach le Iób.*
as patient as Job

Folamh *chomh folamh le sac.*
as empty as a sack

Flúirseach *chomh flúirseach le gaineamh na trá.*
as plentiful as the sand on the beach

Fuar *chomh fuar leis an mbás.*
as cold as death

Gasta *chomh gasta le spideog.*
as fast as a robin

Geal *chomh geal le sneachta.*
as bright as snow

Géar *chomh géar le snáthaid.*
as sharp as a needle

    chomh géar le súil cailín i lár cuideachta.
    as sharp as a girl's eye in the middle of a gathering of people

    (ironically) *chomh géar le bó mhaol.*
    as sharp as a bald cow

Glan *chomh glan le scilling.*
as clean as a shilling

Glic *chomh glic le madra rua.*
as cunning as a fox

Glórach *chomh glórach le cearc ghoir.*
as noisy as a clucking hen

Gránna *chomh gránna le muc.*
as ugly as a pig

Goirt *chomh goirt le sáile.*
as bitter as brine

Gorm *chomh gorm leis an spéir.*
as blue as the sky

Íseal *chomh híseal leis an talamh.*
as low as the ground

Lábánach *chomh lábánach le láib.*
as common as muck

Lag *chomh lag le huisce/le sicín.*
as weak as water/as a chicken

Láidir *chomh láidir le capall.*
as strong as a horse

Lán *chomh lán leis an fharraige.*
as full as the sea

Leamh *chomh leamh le huisce portaigh.*
as dull as ditch-water

Leathan *chomh leathan leis an fharraige.*
as wide as the sea

Leisciúil *chomh leisciúil le hasal.*
as lazy as a donkey

Liath *chomh liath le broc.*
as grey as a badger

Lom *chomh lom le bos mo láimhe.*
as bare as the palm of my hand

Luaineach *chomh luaineach leis an ghaoth Mhárta.*
as fickle as the March wind

Maol *chomh maol le croí mo dhearnan.*
as bald as the hollow of my hand

Macánta *chomh macánta le sagart.*
as honest as a priest

Mall *chomh mall le seilide.*
as slow as a snail

Marbh *chomh marbh le hart.*
as dead as a stone

Meisce *chomh mór ar meisce le bean a' leanna.*
as drunk as a barmaid

Milis *chomh milis le mil.*
as sweet as honey

Mín *chomh mín le síoda.*
as soft as silk

Mínáireach *chomh mínáireach le muc.*
as shameless as a pig

Mion *chomh mion le púdar.*
as fine as powder

Mór *chomh mór le taobh an tí.*
as big/tall as the side of the house

Nimhneach *chomh nimhneach le heasóg.*
as spiteful/venomous as a stoat

   chomh nimhneach le mála easóg.
   as vicious/venomous as a bag of weasels

Pioctha *chomh pioctha le biorán nua.*
as neat/spruce as a new pin

Pollta *chomh pollta le criathar.*
as full of holes as a sieve

Ramhar *chomh ramhar le muc/le ministir.*
as fat as a pig/as a clergyman

Righin *chomh righin le gad.*
as tight as a knot

Saibhir *chomh saibhir le tiarna talún.*
as rich as a landlord

Salach *chomh salach le cró muice.*
as dirty as a pigsty

Sean *chomh sean leis na cnoic (is níos sine faoi dhó).*
as old as the hills (and twice as old again)

Seang *chomh seang le capall rása.*
as slim as a racehorse

Siúráilte *chomh siúráilte le Dia in airde.*
as sure as God is on high

Sleamhain *chomh sleamhain le heireaball eascainne.*
as slippery as the tail of an eel

Smeartha *chomh smeartha le naprún búistéara.*
as smudged as a butcher's apron

Tanaí *chomh tanaí le habhlainn/le cú.*
as thin as a wafer/as a hound

Te *chomh te le tinte ifrinn.*
as hot as the fires of hell

Teann *chomh teann le téad.*
as taut as a rope

Tinn *chomh tinn le neascóid/le gadhar.*
as sick as a boil/as a dog

Tirim *chomh tirim le spríos.*
as dry as tinder
('*spríos*'—dry twigs)

Tiubh *chomh tiubh le dair.*
as thick-set as an oak tree

    chomh tiubh le grean.
    as plentiful/dense as gravel

    chomh tiubh géar le tiul.
    as thick as in a hail/shower
    (i.e. very quickly and densely. cf. *Bhí na ceisteanna ag teacht chomh tiubh le tiul*—The questions were coming thick and fast.)

Trom *chomh trom le luaidhe.*
as heavy as lead

    (of fog) *chomh trom is go n-íosfá le spúnóg é.*
    So thick you could eat it with a spoon.

Conceit (*Mórchúis*)

Seachain fear an uabhair!
Avoid the proud/arrogant man!

Na taoisigh uaibhreacha cá bhfuil siad anois?
The proud chieftains, where are they now?
(N.B. This is based on lines from an '*Amhrán Tíre*':
'*Na taoisigh uaibhreacha a bhí faoi ghradam mór inné; Cá bhfuilid inniu,
arae, faoi leac le cruimheanna cré!*'
'The proud chieftains who were once held in high esteem, where are they
now? Alas, under a flagstone with maggots in the clay.' It is said about
any powerful or important person who is behaving arrogantly and with
disdain to others.)

Bristear long le linn an ghála, t'r éis mórála lucht a tógála.
The ship is lost in the gale after much boasting by its builders.

Meirgí maíte tar éis bheith cloíte.
Proud banners after having been defeated.
(i.e. (i) boasting inappropriately after having been defeated; or
(ii) making the best of a bad outcome)

Titeann maíteach i bpoll.
The boaster falls into a hole.
(cf. Pride comes before a fall.)

Ná maígh tú féin as an lá amárach!
Do not boast about (what you will achieve) tomorrow.

Conscience (*Coinsias*)

Dá olc iardraí an ainghnímh a d'fhulaing is measa fós don té a rinne.
However bad the consequence of the evil deed, it will be worse for the
one who perpetrated it.
(i.e. A bad conscience is the worst punishment.)

Níl codladh lae ná oíche riamh ag daoscar déanta ainghnímh.
There is no sleep day or night for evil-doers.

Coinsias gan smear an sciath is fearr.
A clear conscience is the best protection.

Coinsias glan an adhairt is fearr.
A clear conscience is the best pillow.

*Comhairlíonn an coinsias mar chara ar dtús, ach sa deireadh mar
bhreitheamh do do dhaoradh.*
Conscience counsels as a friend at first, but in the end condemns you
like a judge.
(Stanisław Leszczyński, 1677—1733)

Contentment (*Sástacht*)

Is leor bheith sásta.
To be content is enough.

Is fearr saibhir go sona ná daibhir go dona.
It is better to be rich and happy rather than destitute and miserable.
(This is often used for humorous effect against those who equate happiness with being financially or otherwise less well off. It might be used, for example, as a rebuff to such proverbs as '*Is fearr an tsláinte ná na táinte*'—'Health is better than wealth', etc.)

Níl suaimhneas gan saíocht.
There is no peace without wisdom.
(i.e. It takes wisdom to be content.)

An té atá sásta, is duine saibhir é.
He who is satisfied is rich.

Ní cheannóidh an saol sásamh croí.
Contentment cannot be bought.

Cooperation (*Comhoibriú*)

Is maol gualainn gan bhráthair.
A shoulder is bare without a brother.

Ní neart go teacht le chéile.
There is no strength until we come together.
(cf. Many hands make light work.)

An té nach bhfuil linn tá sé inár n-aghaidh.
He who is not with us is against us.

Is fearr dhá chloigeann ná aon chloigeann amháin.
Two heads are better than one.

Tógann an t-oileán an t-ógánach.
The (whole) island raises the youth.
(i.e. Everyone in a community plays a part in raising the children of that community.)

Níonn lámh lámh eile.
One hand washes the other.
(cf. You scratch my back and I'll scratch yours.)

Courage (*Misneach*)

Is dána gach fear go tulaigh.
Every man is brave till he reaches the battle.

Is buan fear ina dhúiche féin.
Every man is brave in his own back yard.

Níor chaill fear an mhisnigh riamh.
Fortune favours the brave.

Is dána gach madra ina dhoras féin.
Every dog is brave it its own doorway.

Is minic gurb í an eagla máthair an mhisnigh.
Fear is often the mother of courage.

Turas abhaile an bás don té atá cróga.
Death is but going home to the brave.
(Chinese Proverb)

Fásann an misneach le teacht ócáide.
'Courage mounteth with occasion.'
(*King John* (2,1), William Shakespeare, 1582—1616)

Cowardice (*Meatacht*)

Is fearr rith maith ná drochsheasamh.
A good run is better than a bad stand.
(cf. Discretion is the better part of valour.)

Grá mná maithe, meidhir ná maoin—ní bheidh dá leithéidí ag cladhaire díomhaoin.
The love of a good woman, mirth and wealth—will never be acquired by an idle coward.

Druidtear gach geata roimh chroí atá meata.
Every gate closes before a cowardly heart.

Níl beatha ag fear meata ach faigheann sé bás.
The coward had no life, but nonetheless he dies.

Is iomaí bás ag an meatachán.
The coward has many deaths.

Crime (*Coiriúlacht*)

Is í an bhochtaineacht cré na coiriúlachta.
Poverty is the clay of crime.
(i.e. Poverty is the breeding ground for criminality.)

Is é tuarastal don pheacaí bás.
The wages of the sinner is death.
(cf. Crime does not pay.)

Tabhair rogha don bhodach agus tógfaidh sé an díogha.
Let a churl choose and he will choose the worst.

Níl aon mhaith le gnóthú riamh ó ainghníomh.
There is no good ever to be gained from an evil deed.
(cf. Crime does not pay.)

Is é an bás iarmhairtí an pheaca.
Death is the wages of sin.
(i.e. Crime will always bring misfortune and death.)

Taobh thiar de gach saibhreas saolta, gheofar coir áibhéalta.
Behind every worldly fortune, will be found a huge crime.
(i.e. It is impossible to make any vast fortune without instigating an act/
acts of criminality.)

Cad é robáil bainc i gcomparáid le bunú bainc?
What is robbing a bank compared to founding one?
(*The Threepenny Opera* (3,3), Bertolt Brecht, 1858—1956)

Criticism (*Cáineadh*)

Is í an lámh a shíntear an lámh a cháintear.
It is the hand that helps that is criticised.

Ná mol agus ná cáin tú féin.
Do not praise and do not criticise yourself.

Moladh luath agus cáineadh mall.
Be quick to praise and slow to criticise.

Más maith leat do cháineadh, pós!
If you like being criticised, get married!

An pota ag aor ar an gciteal.
The pot satirising the kettle.
(cf. The pot calling the kettle black.)

Cad chuige ar léir duit an dúradán i súil do bhráthar agus gan tú ag tabhairt faoi deara na saile atá i do shúil féin.
Why do you see the mote in your brother's eye and not notice the beam in your own eye?
(Biblical)

Leigheas thú féin, a lia úd!
Physician, heal thyself!
(Biblical. i.e. said to someone who should heed their own advice)

Caitheadh an duine gan aon pheaca an chéad chloch!
Let he who is without sin cast the first stone!
(Biblical: cf. People in glass houses shouldn't throw stones.)

Cures (*Leigheasanna*)

Níl aon leigheas ar an ghrá ach pósadh.
Marriage is the only cure for love.

Bíonn an bás mar leigheas ar an saol.
Death is the cure for life.

An rud nach féidir a leigheas is í an fhoighne is fearr.
What cannot be cured must be endured.

Leigheastar an tuirse le codladh,
Leigheas ar an ghruaim an grá,
Leigheastar an fhearg le moladh,
Leigheas ar an mórtas an gá.

Tiredness is cured by sleep,
The cure for sorrow is love,
Anger is cured by praise,
And arrogance cured by need.

Níl luibh ná leigheas in aghaidh an bháis.
There is no herb or cure against death.

Is measa an leigheas ná an galar féin.
The cure is worse than the disease itself.

Is minic gur fearr luí ná lia liom.
It is often that I would prefer to be sick than to be in a doctor's care.

Níl lia ag an mbocht ach an bás.
There is no doctor for the poor but death.

An té nach leigheasann im ná uisce beatha, níl aon leigheas air.
He whom butter or whiskey cannot cure is incurable.

Leasú seacht mbliana—brúcht mhaith sneachta.
A good fall of snow fertilises the soil for seven years.

Neantóg a dhóigh mé, agus cupóg a leigheas mé.
A nettle stung me and a dock-leaf healed me.
(i.e. There is a natural cure for everything.)

Níl aon mhaitheas le gnóthú riamh ó lucht déanta ainghnímh.
There is no good ever gained from those who commit a wicked deed.
(i.e. Good cannot come from evil.)

Is iad an codladh agus an gáire an dá leigheas is láidre.
Sleep and laughter are the best cures.

Leigheas thú féin, a Lia úd.
Physician, heal thyself.
(Biblical)

Curses (*Mallachtaí*)

Go n-éirí an bóthar fút!
May the road rise up and swallow you!

Imeacht gan teacht ort!
May you go and never return!

Tochas gan sóchas chugat!
May you have an itch that may never be relieved!

Bás na gcat sa dúluachair chugat, bás liath gan bhainne ná ola an tsagairt!
May you die as cats in deepest winter, a grey death without milk or absolution!
(cf. May you die roaring with the leg of a chair in your mouth!)

Do chorp don diabhal!
The devil take you!

Go n-ithe an cat thú agus go n-ithe an diabhal an cat!
May a cat eat you and may the devil eat the cat!

Go gcuire sé sconna ort!
May it give you the runs!

Ná raibh rath ná críoch ort!
May you have neither success nor fulfilment!

Leá mún Mhóire ort!
The melting of Island-woman's urine be on you!
(i.e. May you and your possessions disappear like the melting of Móir's urine. cf. *'An tOileánach' lch. 67*. 'Móir (i.e. the Island-woman) needs to have a pee, having reached Muisire Pass in search of Donncha Daoi, her husband. She decides to choose the road along which the urine travels farthest because she did not know which way to go. But this didn't work out for her because it went the same length along each road. She said: 'Ireland is long and wide. Wasn't it a short distance this narrow stream travelled? I had better return home to my own little abode and to abandon Donncha.' i.e. May you and your possessions disappear as quickly as Móir's urine.)

Go gcuire sé saill ort!
May it make you fat!

Céile leice leisciúil léanmhar chugat!
May your spouse be a lazy, unfortunate idiot!

Ná raibh Ifreann lán go raibh tú ann!
May Hell not be full until you arrive!

Leaba bhán chugat!
A white bed to you!
(i.e. a deathbed)

Go mbeire an Diabhal ort is go mbrise sé do chosa!
May the devil grab you and break your legs!

Sciamh na bhflaitheas ná feicir choíche!
May you never see the beauty of heaven!

Danger (*Contúirt*)

Caladh ar bith le linn an ghála.
Any harbour during a gale.
(cf. any port in a storm)

Aithnítear gaol sa bhearna bhaoil.
Kindred feelings come to the fore in a time of war.
('*an bhearna bhaoil*'—the gap of danger)

Ní fhaigheann cos ina cónaí dada.
Nothing ventured, nothing gained.

Níor cailleadh leath dá ndeachaigh i gcontúirt.
(Not even) half of those who ventured into danger were lost.

An té gur breá leis dainséar, caillfear ann é.
He who loves danger will be lost by it.

Bíodh eagla ort agus ní baol duit.
Be afraid and you'll have nothing to fear.
(i.e. Fear is the best safeguard against danger.)

Ná téigh san uisce mura bhfuil an snámh agat.
Don't go into the water unless you can swim.

Is bádóir oilte gach fear is an fharraige ina clár.
Every man is a skilled boatman in a calm sea.
(i.e. The sea may look harmless but it has many hidden dangers.)

As an choire agus isteach sa tine.
Out of the cauldron, into the fire.
(cf. Out of the frying pan, into the fire.)

Contúirt mhór an creideamh caoch.
Blind belief is dangerous.

Baol dian an béal gan srian.
Unbridled speech is a serious danger.

Leath den ghuais leis an imeacht luais.
A speedy departure will lessen the danger by half.

Ná tabhair don daoirse diúltamh agus tabharfar saoirse duit.
Don't refuse hardship and you will be given freedom.
(i.e. Don't run away from danger or difficulties and you will resolve them.
'Saoirse' by Seán Ó Ríordáin, 1910—1977.)

Death (*An Bás*)

Tagann an bás chuig cách.
Death comes to everyone.

Níl bás go beatha.
There is no death without (first) living.
(This is a less commonly found alternative to: '*Is iomaí lá sa reilig orainn*'—
'It is many the day in the graveyard upon us.' It is used to encourage a
companion or companions to indulge in another drink or to throw caution
to the wind as there is no point in life if one hasn't enjoyed it to the full.)

Geallann gach breith bás.
Every birth promises death.

Níl breith gan bás.
There is no birth that eludes death.
(Often said in reference to a sudden or untimely death.)

Is iomaí lá sa reilig orainne.
It is many a day in the graveyard upon us.
(i.e. So let us enjoy ourselves!)

Creideann do chara agus do namhaid nach bhfaighidh tú bás choíche.
Both your friend and your enemy think you will never die.

Ní sonas seanaois, ní bainis bás.
Old age is not happiness; death is not a wedding.
(i.e. However bad old age is, the alternative is worse.)

Bua na beatha an bás.
The victory of life is death.
(This proverb may have several interpretations. Firstly, after all life's trials and tribulations, death can be seen as a reward; secondly, there is nothing to be gained by being an uncharitable wretch in this life because we all end up in the grave; thirdly, there is nothing better to be wished for in this life but death itself.)

Breith, baisteadh, bean, buaireamh, bás.
Birth, christening, wife/woman, sorrow, death.
(This very old saying about a rather gloomy cycle of life dates back to the time of Peig Sayers, or maybe even earlier. Note that it can be used both by men and women as '*bean*' has the meaning of 'wife' or 'being a woman'.)

Ní rachaidh rachmas chun na huaighe ach rachaidh rún.
Wealth will not go to the grave, but a secret will.
(i.e. We die as we are born—with nothing.)

Ní thabharfaidh tú do chóta chun na huaighe.
You will not bring your coat to the grave.

Is namhaid an bás don óige agus cara don sean.
Death is an enemy of youth and a friend of old age.

Peaca an lae is uaigneas oíche go dtagann an t-éag le suaimhneas choíche.
The sin [i.e. toil] of the day and the loneliness of the night until death comes with eternal peace.
(i.e. Death is a release from the troubles of life. N.B. the internal rhyme in this proverb: ea-é-ea-í: ea-é-ea-í. It is likely that it is a part of an '*Amhrán Tíre*', the rest of which has been lost.)

Níl luibh ná leigheas ina aghaidh an bháis.
There is no herb or medicine to prevent death.

Maireann an chraobh ar an bhfál ach ní mhaireann an lámh a chuir.
The branch lives on the hedge, but not the hand that planted it.
(i.e. What we do in this life is far more permanent than we are.)

Ní bheathaíonn na mairbh an beo.
The dead do not sustain the living.
(i.e. Let us not talk about the dead or about what was in the past—let us concentrate on relevant matters of the day.)

Bíonn an bás ar aghaidh an tseanduine ach ar chúl an duine óig.
Death is in front of the old person but behind the young person.
(i.e. Although old people are expecting death, death may come unexpectedly to the young.)

Níl an bás in imigéin ach aon áit ina bhfuilimid féin.
Death is not far from us but in every place we are.

Níl an t-éag imithe go dtagann an bás.
Death has only gone when it arrives in a new disguise.
(i.e. You think you're over one thing when another equally bad thing happens.)

Is fearr súil le glas ná súil le bás/le huaigh.
It is better to hope for a return from prison than from death/from the grave.

Cothaíonn gráin bás.
Hatred kills.

Is buaine clú ná duine.
Reputation/fame is more lasting than a person is.

Tagann an bás mar ghadaí san oíche.
Death comes like a thief in the night.
(Biblical)

Is bitseach í an saol agus ansin faigheann tú bás.
Life is a bitch and then you die.

Deartháir don bhás an codladh.
Sleep is a brother to death.

Is mairg don té a fhaigheann bás san fhearthainn mar tagann an ghrian amach ina diaidh.
Woe to him who dies in the rain because the sun comes out afterwards.

Téann uasal i gcóiste chun na reilige, téann bochtán i gcairt ach itheann na cruimheanna iad araon.
The noble man goes to the graveyard in a hearse, the poor man on a cart, but the maggots eat them both alike.

Is minic gur fearr bás ná breoiteacht.
It is often that death is preferable to illness.

Bheireann an bás blas don bheatha.
Death gives a taste to life.
(i.e. If life had no end it would lose its value and its enjoyment.)

Níl an bás taobh thiar den sliabh ach cois teallaigh le do thaoibh.
Death is not behind the mountain but at home by your side.
(cf. Russian proverb: Смерть не за горами, а за плечами.)

Debt (*Fiacha*)

Is fearr seanfhiacha ná seanfhala.
Old debts are better that old grudges.

Is fiach má ghealltar.
A promise is a debt.

Ní dhíolann dearmad fiacha.
A debt is still unpaid even if is forgotten.

De dheasca an úis 'tá fiach, ceasna is núis.
Because of usury, there is debt, affliction and bother.

Fiacha amuigh—liacha istigh.
When there are debts out there are tales of woe inside.
(i.e. Debts lead to misery.)

Fásann fiacha gan deoch a thabhairt dóibh.
Debts grow without watering them.

Deeds (*Gníomhartha*)

Is fearr an t-aon ghníomh amháin ná céad focal.
One action is better than a thousand words.

Ní bheathaíonn briathra na bráithre.
The brothers do not live on words.
(i.e. Actions speak louder than words. In this situation, the brothers need people to provide financial support.)

Ní briathar a dhearbhaíos ach gníomh.
It is not a word that proves, but an action.
(cf. Actions speak louder than words.)

Ní dhéanfá choíche dea-ghníomh gan íoc as.
You'd never do a good deed without paying for it.
(cf. No good deed goes unpunished. There is a less common form: '*Ní dhéanfá dea-ghníomh choíche gan éiric a íoc*'—lit. 'You could never do a good deed without paying for it.')

Molann an gníomh é féin.
The deed praises itself.

Defamation (*Aithisiú*)

Is é an clúmhilleadh an t-olc is measa.
Slander is the worst evil.

Is beo duine d'éis na huaighe ach ní beo d'éis a oinigh.
A person lives after death, but is not alive after dishonour.

Is measa fianaise na mbréag ná an t-éag.
False witness is worse than death.

Níl an diabhal chomh dona lena thuairisc.
The devil isn't as bad as his report.
(cf. The Devil isn't as black as he's painted.)

Ná habair olc faoi do chomharsa.
Do not speak evil of your neighbour.

Mura bhfuil le rá faoi dhuine ach grus—ná habair faic ach fan i do thost!
If you only have something unpleasant to say about a person, it's better to say nothing at all.
(*'grus'*—an unpleasant expression, an unkind word)

Is measa caill onóra ná gad an chrochadóra.
Losing one's honour is worse than the hangman's knot.
(cf. He who has been defamed is half-hanged.)

Dá fhad is a bheidh tú amuigh, ná beir drochscéal abhaile ort féin.
However long you are away, never bring any bad news about yourself home.

Glacann dubh dath ach ní ghlacann dath dubh.
Colour takes black, but black doesn't take colour.

Dorn de shó agus lán baile de náire.
A fist full of money is worth a full village of shame.

Loiteann aor beag clú mór.
A small satire destroys a great reputation.

Rachaidh fealltóirí is lucht millte clú go híochtar ifrinn mar is dual.
Traitors and defamers, as is fitting, will go to the pits of hell.

Ná bí ag éisteacht le béadchaint lucht spíde,
Mar ní bhfaighidh tú uathu ach olc is drochíde.
Do not be listening to the gossip of slanderers,
For you will only receive from them evil and abuse.

Daoine a dhéanann béadchaint leat, déanfaidh siad béadchaint fút freisin.
People who gossip with you will also gossip about you.

Delay (*Moill*)

Is fearr déanach ná choíche.
Better late than never.

Ní deabhadh ná é arsa muintir Poimpé.
There is no hurry or the like, said the people of Pompeii.

Moill in aghaidh an deabhaidh.
Delay in spite of hurrying.
(cf. More haste; less speed.)

An rud a théann i bhfad téann sé i bhfuaire.
The thing that goes on for a long time becomes cold.
(cf. Procrastination is the thief of time.)

Mair a chapaill agus gheobhaidh tú féar.
Live horse and you will get grass.
(i.e. telling people who are dying of starvation that all they have to do is
to live and eventually they will get food)

Is fearr treabhadh mall ná gan treabhadh ar bith.
Better to plough late than never to plough.
(cf. Better late than never.)

Tá dhá lá san earrach níos fearr ná deich lá san fhómhar.
Two days in spring is better than ten days in autumn.
(i.e. What is postponed is often more difficult to do.)

Deserving (*Tuillteanas*)

A cheart don té a thuill é.
His due to the one who has earned it.
(cf. Credit where credit is due.)

Is fiú a thuarastal an t-oibrí.
The labourer is worthy of his hire.
(Biblical)

Filleann an feall ar an bhfeallaire.
The evil deed returns upon the evildoer.

Muileann muilte Dé go mall ach muileann siad go mion mín.
The mills of God grind slowly, but they grind exceedingly fine.
(i.e. Justice may be slow, but it will come eventually.)

An té a chuireann san earrach bainfidh sé san fhómhar.
He who sows in spring shall reap in autumn.

Destiny (*Cinniúint*)

Níl éalú ón chinniúint.
There is no escaping destiny.

An rud atá le teacht, tiocfaidh sé.
What is to come will come.
(cf. What must be must be.)

An rud atá i ndán ní bheimid gan.
The thing that is fated to be, we shall not avoid.

Má tá sé i ndán dom crochadh ní bháfar mé.
If I am fated to be hanged; I shall not drown.
(cf. He who has an appointment with the gallows shall not drown.)

Bíonn a bhóithrín féin ag gach duine.
Everyone has their own road to travel.

Is minic go mbuaileann ár gcinniúint linn ar na bóithre úd gur thógamar chun éalú uaithi.
It is often that we meet our destiny on the very roads we took to avoid it.
(Cf. '*On rencontre sa destine—Souvent par des chemins qu'on prend pour l'éviter.*' Jean de La Fontaine, 1621—1695)

Devil (*An Diabhal*)

Is fearr an diabhal abhus ná an diabhal anall.
The devil you know is better than the devil you don't.

Is diabhal bean ar bith gan fear maith.
Any woman is a devil without a good man.

Ar uaire bíonn an fhírinne i mbéal an diabhail.
Sometimes the truth is on the lips of the devil.

Má tá an paróiste faoi bhagairt is diabhal an sagart.
If the parish is under threat then the priest is a devil.
(i.e. When it's a matter of life or death, even gentle people can show a savage side.)

Níl an diabhal i sléibhte Uíbh Fhaillí ach i lúb na cuideachta mhuintir cois teallaigh.
The devil isn't in the mountains of Offaly but at home amidst our kin.

Is gnóthach an diabhal i mbothán díomhaoin.
The devil is busy in an idle man's house.
(cf. The devil finds work for idle hands.)

Nuair a ghabhann Dia an doras amach, tagann an diabhal gan cuireadh isteach.
When God does out the door, the devil comes in without an invitation.

Nuair nach n-éisteann Dia lenár nguí, éistfidh an Diabhal.
When God will not listen to our prayers, the devil will.
(i.e. used to imply that if something cannot be achieved by fair means then foul means will be employed)

Diligence (*Dúthracht*)

Is fearr díomhaoin ná dúthracht gan dearcadh.
It is better to be idle than to act mistakenly with zeal.

Dúthracht is dícheall a thug fairsing go fial.
Zeal and diligence provided generous plenty.

Déan rud amháin agus déan go maith é.
Do one thing and do it well.

Rith i ndiaidh triúir agus fill le mála folamh.
Run after three and come back with an empty bag.

Is deacair bua a fháil ar an duine nach ngéillfidh choíche.
It is difficult to beat a person who will never give up.

Ní bhfaighfeá aicearra choíche go háit arbh fhiú dul ann.
There are no shortcuts to any place worth going.
(Beverly Sills, 1929—2007)

Discipline (*Smacht*)

Ní bhíonn an rath ach mar a mbíonn an smacht.
There is no success but where there is discipline.
(This is often used as an equivalent for the Biblical expression: 'Spare the rod and spoil the child' (Proverbs 13:24). However, although the beating of children occurred in Gaelic Ireland, it was always considered a shameful thing to do and never spoken about in public.)

Tabhair páiste dom ar feadh seacht mbliana, agus is féidir do rogha rud a dhéanamh leis ina dhiaidh sin.
Give me a child for the first seven years, and I will give you the man.
(This is a statement attributed to the Jesuits of Ireland, who believed that a child's mind could be easily indoctrinated at an early age. It was widely held that whatever had been taught in the early years of life could not be fundamentally altered by any later educational experience.)

Ní féidir le rí smacht a choimeád mura bhfuil smacht aige air féin.
A king can only keep discipline if he can remain disciplined himself.

Ní bhíonn slacht ach san áit a mbíonn an smacht.
For things to look good, there needs to be discipline.

Tagann foghlaim an smachta ó thuistí á chleachtadh.
The learning of discipline (by children) comes from parents practising it.

Discretion (*Discréid*)

Ná bac le mac an bhacaigh agus ní bhacfaidh mac ann bhacaigh leat.
Do not bother the son of the tramp and the son of the tramp will not
bother you.

Dearc roimh léim a thabhairt!
Look before you leap!

Moladh gach aon an t-áth mar a gheobhaidh.
Let each man praise the ford as he finds it.

Breith anabaí breith bhaoth.
A premature judgement is a foolish one.

Ná tabhair do bhreith ar an gcéad scéal!
Don't pass judgement on the first story!
(i.e. Don't rush to conclusions before hearing both sides of the argument.)

Is fusa snaidhm a chur ná a bhaint.
It is easier to make a knot than to undo it.

Soir gach siar faoi dheireadh thiar.
East is west when you're far enough west.
(cf. Extremes meet.)

Is fearr rith maith ná drochsheasamh.
A good run is better than a bad stand!
(cf. Discretion is the better part of valour.)

Ná cuir an sionnach ag buachailleacht na gcaorach.
Don't put the fox to look after the sheep.

Déan do thine duit féin—agus ná bí ag brath ar do ghoradh ag an ngréin.
Make your own fire—and do not depend on warming yourself by the sun.

An rud nach féidir an rud is fearr.
The thing that is impossible is always the best.

Is deacair droim ina haonar leis an bhfarraige mhór.
One single back against the open sea is difficult.
(i.e. One person or a handful of people cannot stop the inevitable.)

Níl saoi gan locht.
There isn't a wise man without his fault.

Tá fáth ag gach rud.
There is a reason for everything.

Ná tóg aníos mé go dtitim síos.
Don't pick me up before I fall down.
(i.e. Don't fuss over me; let me do it on my own, etc.)

Ná cuir do ghob i gcuideachta gan iarraidh.
Don't stick your beak into company without being asked.

Bíonn eagla na tine ar leanbh dóite.
A burnt child is afraid of fire.
(cf. Once bitten, twice shy.)

Ní scéal rúin a chuala triúr.
A story isn't secret when three have heard it.

Is fearr fuíoll ná easnamh.
It is better to have too much than to have too little.
(cf. It is better to err on the safe side.)

Ná bain an tuí de do theach féin le sclátaí a chur ar theach eile.
Don't take the thatch off your own house in order to put tiles on another man's house.

Ná bris do lorga ar stól nach bhfuil sa tslí ort.
Don't break you shin on a stool that isn't in your way.
(i.e. Don't make unnecessary problems for yourself.)

Níor tháinig fear na headrána saor riamh.
The mediator of a dispute never got off scot-free.
(i.e. The mediator often becomes involved in the dispute.)

Más maith leat síocháin, cairde agus moladh—éist, féach agus fan balbh!
If you want peace, friendship and praise—listen, look and remain dumb!

Más maith leat do mholadh—faigh bás.
If you want praise—die!
(i.e. People usually do not speak well of the living or ill of the dead.)

Dress (*Feisteas*)

Feisteas galánta ar chailleach chadránta.
Elegant dress on a callous old hag.
(cf. mutton dressed as lamb)

Is álainn más aosta an té atá gléasta.
Even an old person can look well dressed up.

Culaith ghaisce ar laoch in aisce.
Heroic dress upon a warrior that is wanting.
(i.e. all talk and no substance)

Buailtear le daoine ar a n-éadach ach tionlactar iad ar a gcomhrá.
We meet people because of their attire, but we accompany them on account of their conversation.

Is é an duine an t-éadach.
A person is the clothes (they wear).
(cf. Clothes maketh the man.)

Is giorra do dhuine a léine ná a chóta.
A person's shirt is closer to them than their coat.
(cf. Blood is thicker than water.)

114

Drinking (*Ólachán/Ól*)

Deartháir don ghadaíocht an t-ólachán.
Robbery is the brother of drinking.

Is milis fíon ach is searbh a íoc.
Wine is sweet but sour its payment.

Sceitheann fíon fírinne.
Wine releases the truth.

Ní cuireadh gan deoch.
It isn't an invitation without a drink.

Is giorra deoch ná scéal.
A drink comes before a story.

Is maith an bhean chaointe buidéal líonta.
A full bottle is a good 'wailing woman'.
(*'bean chaointe'*—wailing woman, a woman hired to weep loudly at a
wake/funeral. The proverb suggests that a full bottle of alcohol will be
just as effective.)

Drunkenness (*Meisciúlacht*)

Sceitheann fíon fírinne.
Wine releases the truth/loosens the tongue.

An uair a bhíonn an deoch istigh bíonn an chiall amuigh.
When drink is in, sense is out.

Beag an sochar ón síor-mheisce.
There is little profit from being constantly drunk.

Nach ionann meisceoir agus pótaire?!
A drunkard is the same as a drunk.
(i.e. Calling something by a different name does not change its nature.)

Lá ar meisce agus lá ag ól uisce.
A day being drunk and (the following) day drinking water.

Tart madaidh ar lá fliuch leithscéal meisceora a lorgaíonn deoch.
A dog's thirst on wet day is the drunkard's excuse when looking for a drink.
(i.e. A false reason to have a drink.)

Baineann an druncaeir an díon dá thigh féin,
agus cuireann sé ar thigh and tábhairne é.
The drunk takes the roof off his own house,
and puts it on the roof of the pub.

Education/Training
(*Oideachas/Oiliúint*)

Is treise nádúr/dúchas ná oiliúint.
Nature is stronger than nurture.

Is deacair cleas nua a mhúineadh do sheanmhadra.
It's hard to teach an old dog new tricks.

Nuair a chruann an tslat is deacair í a lúbadh.
When a twig grows it is hard to bend it.
(i.e. It is easier to learn when young.)

Namhaid ceird mura gcleachtar.
A trade is an enemy if it is not practised.
(cf. Practice makes perfect.)

Is trom an t-ualach aineolas.
Ignorance is a heavy burden.

Ní ualach an t-oideachas ach is ualach mór an t-aineolas.
Education is no burden, but ignorance is a heavy one.

Is éigean don leanbh lámhacán roimh shiúl.
A child has to crawl before it walks.

Effort (*Stró*)

Cúram naonúir ar an mbean gan leanbh.
The childless woman looking after nine.

Obair mhór a bhain an fómhar.
Hard work reaped the harvest.

Ní bhfaighfeá aicearra choíche go háit arbh fhiú dul ann.
There are no shortcuts to any place worth going.
(Beverly Sills, 1929—2007)

Más fiú é a dhéanamh, is fiú é a dhéanamh go maith.
If it is worth doing, it is worth doing well.

An duine a chuireann a dhroim leis an obair, cuirfidh sé a bhéal lena toradh.
A person who puts his back into the work will taste its reward.
(i.e. an invitation to help with some task)

Tógadh gach fear sa naomhóg a sheal ag na maidí rámha.
Let every man in the currach take his turn at the oars.
('currach'—A small wooden-framed boat with a tarred covering that was locally made and used for fishing.)

Evil (*Olc*)

Is fearr olc a fhulaingt ná olc a dhéanamh.
It is better to suffer evil than to do it.

Is olc an ghaoth nach séideann do dhuine éigin.
It is an evil wind that doesn't blow to someone's benefit.

Ní thig olc i dtír nach fearrde duine éigin.
Evil does not come ashore without benefiting someone.

Fada iarsma an drochbhirt.
Long is the aftermath of the evil deed.

Níos lú ná dúradán deannaigh foinse an oilc.
Smaller than a speck of dust is the source of evil.

Níl leigheas ar an olc ach grá Dé.
The only cure for evil is the love of God.

Experience *(Taithí/Cleachtadh)*

Scuabann scuab úr go glan, ach tá fios ag an seanscuab ar na coirnéil.
A new broom sweeps clean, but an old one knows the corners.
(i.e. The experienced person knows things that a new person cannot.)

Éalaímid ó dhéanamh botún de bharr taithí agus tagann an taithí ó dhéanamh botún.
We know how to avoid mistakes from experience, and we get that experience by making mistakes.
(cf. 'Good judgement comes from experience … and experience? … Well that comes from poor judgement.' Rita Mae Brown, 1944—)

Is í an ghaois an duais a bhronntar ar lucht sáraithe a ndíth céille féin.
Wisdom is the prize for those who survive their own stupidity.

Foghlaimítear gach ceird i dtaithí na hoibre.
Every trade is learnt from the experience of doing the work.

Is maith an t-oide an taithí.
Experience is a good teacher.

Faighimid an taithí is fearr ó na botúin a dhéanaimid.
We get our best experience from the mistakes we make.

Fame (*Cáil*)

An té atá thuas óltar deoch dó an té; atá thíos buailtear cos faoi.
The one who is doing well receives a toast; the one who is down is kicked.

Is buaine bláth ná beatha.
Fame is more enduring than life.

Fanann an ród ach fir a dhéanta sínte faoin bhfód.
The road remains, but the men who made it are under the sod.

Is uaisle clú ná ór.
Reputation is more precious than gold.

Loiteann aoir ghearr clú fada.
A short satire destroys a long-held reputation.

Is fearr le cailín cleasaí clúiteach ná an saothraí ciúin dúthrachtach.
A famous trickster is of more interest to a girl than a quiet, diligent worker.
(i.e. Women find fame a very attractive trait in a young man.)

Faigheann an laoch bás ach maireann a cháil go deo.
The hero dies, but his fame lives forever.

Is fuar an clú gan chara.
Fame is a cold thing without a friend.

121

Family (*Clann*)

Is mac mo mhac go bpósfaidh sé. Ach is iníon m'iníon go dtéim i gcré.
My son is my son till he gets a wife. My daughter's my daughter for the rest of my life.

Ní pósadh go clann.
Married is when children arrive.
(Many farmers married late, and occasionally would require confirmation that the woman they were to wed could bear children for them (i.e. by becoming pregnant) before finally concluding the marriage contract.)

Lánúin gan chlann—lán gruaime a mbeann.
A couple who cannot have children—theirs is a horn full of sorrow.

Is fearr liom clann mhac ach is fearr dom clann iníonacha.
I prefer sons, but I'm better off with daughters.

Síleann gach éan gurb í a chlann féin is deise sa choill.
Every bird thinks its own young are the finest in the wood.

Faults (*Lochtanna*)

Is é a locht a laghad.
Its only defect is that there isn't enough of it.

Ní bhíonn saoi gan locht.
There isn't a wise man without flaws.

Ní fheiceann éinne a lochtanna féin.
No one sees their own faults.

Tá siad fíor-mhaith iad siúd atá gan locht.
(ironically) They are really very good those who are without fault.

Aithníonn cú géar a lochtanna féin.
A sharp hound recognises its own faults.

Is iomaí cron a fheictear i nduine bocht.
It is many the fault that is seen in a poor person.

Cad chuige ar léir duit an dúradán i súil do bhráthar agus gan tú ag tabhairt faoi deara na saile atá i do shúil féin.
Why do you see the mote in your brother's eye and not notice the beam in your own eye?
(Biblical)

Fear (*Eagla*)

Bíodh eagla ort agus ní baol duit.
Be afraid and you have nothing to fear.

Déanann an eagla bithiúnach den fhear macánta.
Fear makes a scoundrel of a honest man.

Tosach na gaoise eagla an Tiarna.
The beginning of wisdom is the fear of the Lord.
(Biblical)

Is cuid den ghaois an eagla.
Fear is a part of wisdom.

Is treise eagla ná grá.
Fear is stronger than love.

Máthair na seifte an eagla.
The mother of resourcefulness is fear.

Lia na heagla an t-eolas.
The cure for fear is knowledge.

Fighting/Struggle (*Troid/Coimhlint*)

Is fearr an troid ná an t-uaigneas.
Fighting is better than loneliness.

Cloíonn neart ceart.
Might is right.

Is treise gliceas ná neart.
Cunning is better than strength.
(i.e. Clever thinking can avoid resorting to a physical struggle.)

Ní slua neach ina aonar.
One man on his own isn't an army.
(cf. You and whose army?)

D'fhear cogaidh comhalltar síocháin.
Prepare for war to keep the peace.

Iomad lámh a bhaineann an cath.
It is a multitude of hands that wins the battle.
(cf. Many hands make light work.)

Is crua an cath ó nach dtagann fear inste scéil.
It is a tough battle from which none returns to tell the tale.

Troid na mbó maol.
The fight of hornless cows.
(i.e. harmless fight)

Ná seachain agus ná hagair cath.
Do not avoid and do not provoke a battle.

Is fearr deireadh fleá na tús bruíne.
The end of a feast is better than the start of strife.

Druid le fear bruíne agus gheobhaidh tú síocháin.
Face up to the trouble-maker and you will have peace.

Is olc bua na bruíne ach is measa a díomua.
Winning a quarrel is bad, but losing it is worse.
(i.e. Nothing is ever gained by quarrelling over things.)

Bíonn marú an duine idir dhá fhocal.
The killing of a man may be between two words.
(i.e. Choose your words wisely.)

Téann focal le gaoth ach téann buille le cnámh.
A word goes to the wind, but a blow goes to the bone.
(i.e. One might overlook a cross word, but physical violence has more serious and lasting consequences. cf. Sticks and stones may break my bones but words will never hurt me.)

Is éasca deargadh ar aithinne a fhorloscadh.
It is easy to enkindle a burning ember.

Luífidh iolra ar uatha.
The many oppress the few.

Flattery (*Plámás*)

Dearth *don bhréag an béal bán.*
Flattery is next to lying.

An fhírinne caite amach as an tigh ach suíonn an plámás i bparlús an rí.
Truth is thrown out of the house while flattery sits in the king's parlour.

Níonn lámh lámh eile.
One hand washes another.
(cf. You scratch my back I'll scratch yours.)

Tabharfaidh do theanga chun na Róimhe thú.
Your tongue will bring you to Rome.
(i.e. The gift of the gab will get you a long way in this world.)

Bladair an drochmhadra agus ní heagal duit an deamhadra.
Soft-soap the wicked dog and you need not fear the good dog.
(i.e. Mollify the wicked and you need not fear the strong.)

Osclóidh an plámás dúnta na hÉireann duit.
Flattery will open the forts of Ireland.
(cf. Flattery will get you everywhere.)

Déanann bladar cairdeas.
Flattery creates friendship.

Ní cara gach bladaire.
Every flatterer is not a friend.

Cineál ómóis aithris lom.
Barefaced copying is a kind of respect.
(cf. Imitation is the sincerest form of flattery.)

Deirtear gur dual don amadán
A bheith ag éisteacht le béal bán,
Ach uaireanta is maith le saoi
Focal nó dhó ó phlámásaí.
It is an old maxim in the schools,
That flattery's the food of fools,
Yet now and then your men of wit,
Will condescend to take a bit.
(Jonathan Swift, 1667—1745)

Bia an amadáin briathra an bhéil bháin
Flattery is the food of the fool.

Buann an bladaireacht aon rud is mian leat.
Flattery will get you anything.

Food and Drink (*Bia agus Deoch*)

Nua gach bia agus sean gach deoch.
Food should be fresh and drink aged.

Ní miste don lón dul chun aistir.
Lunch doesn't mind taking on a journey.
(i.e. A person who has eaten well is ready undertake physical work.)

Ní béile bia gan deoch.
A meal isn't a meal without a drink.

Is minic a mhaolaigh béile maith brón.
It is often a good meal took the edge off sorrow.

Rud a íosfaidh duine amháin, maróidh sé duine eile.
A thing that one person will eat will kill another.

Ní mhaireann na bráithre ar bhriathra.
The brothers do not live on words.

Níl cuimhne ar arán a itheadh inné.
Eaten bread is soon forgotten.

Is minic a bhíonn an t-úll dearg go holc ina chroí.
It is often that the red apple is bad in its core.
(i.e. Appearances can be deceptive.)

Lá millte na móna lá fómhar an chabáiste.
The rain that destroys the turf can cause cabbage to grow.
(i.e. What is bad for one thing is good for another. cf. One man's meat is another man's poison.)

Is fearr leathbhairín ná bheith gan arán.
Half a loaf is better than being without bread.

Is é bia capall na hoibre.
Food is the horse of work.
(cf. An army marches on its stomach.)

Is túisce deoch ná scéal.
A drink comes before a story.
(i.e. You should offer a drink before asking for news.)

Trí riachtanas don seanduine liath—bia, deoch agus leaba chun luí.
Three requirements for old age—food, drink, and a bed to lie on.

Foolishness (*Baois*)

Is fusa sparán amadáin a scaoileadh.
It is easy to open a fool's purse.

Mian amadáin an díomhaointeas.
Laziness is a fool's desire.

Aithníonn óinseach amadán.
A foolish woman recognises a fool.

Ritheann an t-ádh go dtí an t-amadán ach ní aithníonn an t-amadán é.
Luck runs to the fool, but the fool does not recognise it.

Bíonn an t-ádh ar amadáin.
Fools have luck.

Níl aon amadán mar sheanamadán.
There is no fool like an old fool.

Amaidí mhór a leanann amaidí bheag.
Great folly follows sweet nothings.

An té a bhíonn ag amaidí ar maidin bíonn sé ag caoineadh um thráthnóna.
He who is acting the fool in the morning is weeping by the afternoon.

Amaideacht ghearr is fearr.
The less folly the better.

Ceann mór na céille bige.
A big head has little sense.

131

'Briseadh gach duine a fhuinneog féin,' mar a dúirt an t-amadán.
As the fool said, 'Let every man break his own window.'

Saol an mhadra bháin ag páistí agus amadáin.
Children and fools have a great life.

Lochán saibhris ina thuile a thug an t-ainniseoir chun buile.
Too much wealth causes madness/folly.

Dealg láibe nó focal amadáin.
A fool's remark is like a thorn in the mud.

Bíonn leigheas ar an duine tinn ach ní ar an amaidí ó bhroinn.
An ill person may be cured, but there is no cure for congenital stupidity.

Is cúis gháire amaidí na hóige ach is cúis náire í sa tseanaois.
The foolishness of youth makes us laugh, but in old age it is a cause of embarrassment.

An bhean gur leasc léi óinseach a dhéanamh di féin, ní bheidh éacht ná gaisce in ndán di choíche.
The woman who is unwilling to look foolish will never achieve greatness.
(cf. 'Until you're ready to look foolish, you'll never have the possibility of being great.'
Cher (Cherilyn Sarkisian), 1946—)

Foresight (*Fadcheann*)

Is maith an aire an fhógairt.
Forewarned is forearmed.

Is den imirt an coimeád.
Part of the game is being on your guard.

Amharc romhat sula dtabharfaidh tú léim!
Look before you leap!

Ná fág sionnach i mbun caorach.
Don't leave a fox guarding sheep.

Is fearr filleadh as lár an átha ná bá sa tuile.
It is better to return from the middle of the ford than to drown in the flood.

Is fearr súil romhat ná dhá shúil i do dhiaidh.
One eye in front of you is better than two eyes behind you.

Forgiveness (*Maithiúnas*)

Ní saol é gan mhaitheamh.
There is no life without forgiveness.

An té nach maitheann ás, níl roimhe ach an bás.
He who does not forgive has only death ahead of him.
(i.e. We cannot get on with our own lives without forgiveness.)

Is cuid den saol an maithiúnas.
Forgiving is a part of life.

Maitheas agus bua ó mhaitheamh croí is trua.
Property and victory from forgiveness and compassion.

Dúchas duine peacú scaitheamh ach ó Dhia beannacht lena mhaitheamh.
It is human nature to sin, but it is a God's blessing to forgive it.
(cf. To err is human; to forgive, divine.)

Friendship (*Cairdeas*)

Is fearr argóint a chailleadh ná cara.
It's better to lose an argument than a friend.

Is fearr cara sa chúirt ná ór sa sparán.
A friend in court is better than gold in your purse.

Is fearr namhaid ná cara cam.
An enemy is better than a crooked friend.

Aithnítear cairde i gcruatan.
Friends are recognised in difficult times.
(cf. A friend in need is a friend indeed.)

Ní easpa go díth carad.
There is no want compared to a lack of friends.

Ná tréig do chara ar do chuid.
Don't abandon your friend for personal advantage.

Is maith an scáthán súil charad.
A friend's eye is a good mirror.

Inis dom cé hiad do chairde agus inseoidh mé duit cé tú féin.
Tell me who your friends are and I shall tell you who you are.

Tástáil do dhuine muinteartha sula dteastóidh sé uait.
Test a friend before you need him.

Deireadh cumainn comhaireamh.
The end of friendship is reckoning.
(i.e. When friends begin to discuss who is giving more or less to the other, the friendship is drawing to its close.)

Níl grá ar bith ann ag fear ar bith is mó ná seo, an fear a thabharfadh a anam ar son a chairde.
Greater love hath no man than this: that a man lay down his life for his friends.
(Biblical)

Ná téigh i muinín carad nua ná sean-namhad.
Do not trust a new friend or an old enemy.

Creideann do chara agus do namhaid nach bhfaighidh tú bás choíche.
Both your friend and your enemy think that you will never die.

Amhail an fíon is fearr, feabhsaíonn cumann le haois.
Like the best wine, friendship improves with age.

Is é dán na gcairde scaradh.
Friends must part.

Giorraíonn beirt bóthar.
Two shorten the road.

Is maol gualainn gan bhráthair.
It's a bare shoulder without a friend.

Aithníonn ciaróg ciaróg eile.
One beetle recognises another.

Is neamhbhuan cogadh na gcarad; má bhíonn sé crua, ní bhíonn sé fada.
Fighting between friends is a temporary thing; if it is bitter, it is never long.

Má bhíonn tú ar lorg carad gan locht, beidh tú gan cara go deo.
If you are looking for a friend without a fault you will never have a friend.

Ní haithne go haontíos.
You don't know someone until you live with them.

Iomad den aithne a mhéadaíonn an tarcaisne.
Familiarity breeds contempt.

In am an ghátair a bhraitear an bráthair / an cairdeas.
In the time of need, friendship is perceived.
(cf. A friend in need is a friend indeed.)

Siúlann fíorchara isteach nuair a shiúlann an chuid eile amach.
A true friend walks in when the rest walk out.

Is í an tseoid is fearr ná an cara dílis.
The best treasure is a faithful friend.

Is iad ár gcairde cúram Dé i riocht cré.
Our friends are God caring for us in human form.

Gain (*Tairbhe*)

Cad é an tairbhe é do dhuine seilbh a fháil ar an domhan ar fad, agus a bheatha féin a chailleadh.
What does it profit a man if he gains the whole world but loses his life?
(This is a slight variation on a Biblical quote: Mark 8:36 '*Cad é an tairbhe é do dhuine seilbh a fháil ar an domhan ar fad, agus seilbh ar a bheatha féin a chailleadh.*')

Níl pá gan chrá.
No wages without toil.
(cf. No pain, no gain!)

Níor dhruid Dia doras amháin gan doras eile a oscailt.
God never closed one door without opening another.
(i.e. There is never a great loss without some gain.)

Ní bhíonn tairbhe saoil i margadh ar bith leis an diabhal.
There is no worldly gain in making a deal with the devil.

Is minic an rud nach mbíonn toirtiúil, tairbheach.
It is often the thing that is not bulky is beneficial.
(i.e. The best goods come in small parcels.)

Gambling (*Cearrbhachas*)

Triúr nach féidir a leigheas—pótaire, slataire agus cearrbhach.
Three people who cannot be cured—the drinker, the womaniser and the gambler.

Tá teach an chearrbhachais ar an ród go hifreann.
The gamblers' den is on the road to hell.

Is fearr mac le himirt ná mac le hól.
A son given to gambling is better than a son given to drink.

Is maith an cearrbhach an diabhal.
The devil is a good card-player.

Súil le cúiteamh do lomann an cearrbhach.
It's the hope of requital that fleeces the gambler.

Is minice cearrbhach gan cártaí ná taoscaire gan scéal.
A gambler without cards is more likely than a drunk without a story.

Generosity (*Féile*)

An ceart roimh an bhféile.
Justice before generosity.

Is é croí na féile fáilte chaoin.
The heart of generosity is a kind welcome.

Ní mhaireann na bráithre ar bhriathra.
The brothers (i.e. monks) do not live on words.
(i.e. Be generous!)

Ní dheachaigh fial riamh go teach an diabhail.
A generous person never went to hell.

Is móide is beannaithe bheith ag tabhairt uait ná ag bailiú chugat.
It is more blessed to give than to receive.
(Biblical)

A mbailímid chú'inn a chaillfidh a shnó, ach a dtugaimid uainn—a bheidh linne go deo.
What we keep will lose its lustre, but what we give away will shine [lit. with us] forever.

Is réidh le gach duine faoi chraiceann dhuine eile.
Everyone is generous with another man's skin.

Gluttony (*Craos*)

Bíonn ocras i gcónaí ar an chraosaire.
The glutton is always hungry
(i.e. His aim of being satisfied ever eludes him.)

Is deartháir don tsuthaireacht an t-otrachán.
Gluttony is the brother of obesity.

Is marfaí craos ná claíomh.
Gluttony is more deadly than the sword.

Saolaíonn suthaireacht saoth síoraí gan sásamh.
Gluttony brings constant suffering and no satisfaction.

Tá bolg sagairt ar an gheimhreadh. (i. geimhreadh an-domhain)
Winter has the belly of a priest. (i.e. a very deep winter)
(Russian saying: 'У зимы поповское брюхо.')

God (*Dia*)

Is giorra cabhair Dé ná an doras.
God's help is closer than the door.

Níor dhruid Dia bearna amháin gan bearna eile a oscailt.
God never closed one gap without opening another.

Níor ordaigh Dia riamh béal gan bia.
God never ordained a mouth to be without food.

Cabhraíonn Dia leo siúd a chabhraíonn leo féin.
God helps those who help themselves.

Roinneann Dia na suáilcí.
God shares out good things.

Níor chuir Dia sceach i mbéal an chuain riamh.
God never put a thorn-bush in the mouth of a harbour.
(i.e. God never stopped the wheels of progress.)

Ní bhíonn Dia le mí-rún daoine.
God takes no part in the evil designs of people.

Ní hé gach aon duine gur ordaigh Dia spúnóg airgid ina bhéal.
God didn't order a silver spoon in every person's mouth.

Goodness (*Maitheas*)

Déan an mhaith in aghaidh an oilc.
Return good for evil.

An rud nach dtéann chun maitheasa, téann sé chun olcais.
The thing that is not improving is getting worse.
(i.e. Nothing remains the same.)

Ní bhíonn tréan buan.
Good things don't last.

Grá Dé stiúir gach maitheasa.
Every good thing is directed by the love of God.

Imíonn an scéimh ach fanann an maitheas.
Beauty fades but goodness remains.

Ní hé an mhaith a bhí ach an mhaith atá.
It is not the good that was but the present good that matters.

Bíonn maitheas Dé níos giorra ná an doras.
God's goodness is closer than the door.

Gossip (*Béadán*)

An áit ina mbíonn an toit bíonn an tine.
There is no smoke without fire.

Bíonn cluasa ar na claíocha.
There are ears on the ditches.
(cf. The walls have ears.)

Is ionann béadán agus bréag.
Lies and gossip are the same thing.

Scéal a théann ó bhéal go cluas, téann sé ó Shamhain go Bealtaine.
A story that is passed from mouth to ear (i.e. gossip) grows in the telling.

Inis do mhnaoi agus inis don inis.
Tell a woman a story and tell the Island.
(cf. 'Telegram, telephone, tell a woman.')

Coinníonn triúr rún má tá beirt acu marbh.
Three keep a secret if two of three are dead.

Is comhchoirithe iad cluas agus béal.
Ear and mouth are accomplices.
(cf. 'Where there are no hearers there are no backbiters.')

Is gadaí agus dúnmharfóir an cúlchainteoir.
The backbiter is a thief and a murderer.
(i.e. Backbiting and gossip can precipitate dreadful consequences.)

Gratitude (*Buíochas*)

Is searbh an t-arán atá ite.
Eaten bread is soon forgotten.

Is fearr buíochas brothallach ná féirín fuar.
Warm gratitude is better than a cold present.

Is géar blas an diomaíochais.
It is bitter the taste of ingratitude.

Is fearr faic ná spraic.
Nothing (said) is better than an admonishment.
(i.e. No word of thanks may be bad, but we may be thankful that at least
we aren't being scolded.
'spraic'—scolding)

Is fearr daba ná dada.
A dollop is better than nothing.
(i.e. A small amount of food or something required is better than nothing.)

Greatness (*Mórgacht*)

Dá airde an sliabh titeann an bháisteach air.
However high the mountain, rain falls upon it.

Titeann fear mór níos crua ná fear beag.
A great man falls harder than an unimportant man.
(cf. The higher they climb, the farther they fall.)

Is minic don té nach mór go mbíonn an mór ann.
It is often the one that is not great is boastful.

Cáil mhór crá mór.
Great reputation is a huge torment.

Saol fónta é bheith in eagla roimh mhórgacht Dé.
It is a worthwhile life that is (spent) in fear/awe of God's greatness.

Is mór iad na beaganna i dteannta a chéile.
They are great all the little things added together.
(i.e. Greatness comes from a lot of small good things we have done.)

Greed (*Saint*)

Is measa saint cumhachta ná saint chun saibhris.
Greed for power is worse than greed for money.

Tréigeann an santachán sásamh an tsaoil.
The greedy person loses the joy of life.

Déanann an grabálaí grabhróga dá shaol.
The grasping person makes crumbs of their life.

Tá an bhochtaineacht sa cheann, ní sa phóca.
Poverty is in the head, not in the pocket.
(cf. He is not poor who has little but he that desires much.)

Is gnáth santachán i riachtanas.
A greedy person is always in need.

Saint bun gach oilc.
Greed is the basis of all evil.
(Biblical)

Habit (*Cleachtadh/Nós*)

Is snáithín nós i dtús a chleachtaidh ach slabhra cuibhrithe sa deireadh thiar.
A habit is a thread at first but a chain in the end.

Ná déan nós agus ná bris nós.
Don't make a custom or break a custom.

Is deacair seanmhadra/seanchapall a bhriseadh as seanchleachtadh.
It's difficult to break an old dog/horse out of an old habit.
(cf. Old habits die hard.)

Fanann na cleachtaí a fhoghlaimímid inár n-óige linn go deo.
The habits that we learn in our youth remain with us forever.

Is deacair sean-nós a bhriseadh.
Old habits die hard.

Níl aon aois nárbh fhéidir drochnós a bhriseadh.
There is no age at which you can't break a bad habit.

Happiness (*Sonas*)

Ná cuir an sonas ar athlá!
Don't postpone joy!

Gáire geal an leigheas is fearr.
Happy laughter is the best medicine.

Is sona an bhean a phósann mac na máthar mairbhe.
Happy is the woman who marries the son of the dead mother.
(i.e. Because there is no mother-in-law to worry about!)

Comharsana béil dorais sonas agus brón.
Joy and sorrow are next-door neighbours.

Ní sonas seanaois, ní bainis bás.
Old age isn't happiness; death isn't a wedding.

Ní bhíonn an sonas gan an donas orlaí tríd.
There is no happiness but that unhappiness inches through it.
(cf. '*Et in Arcadia Ego*'—'I am even in Arcadia' (spoken by Death). Even in the midst of happiness, sorrow is close by. This is the title of a painting by Poussin that depicts shepherds surrounding a tomb. The same words begin Evelyn Waugh's *Brideshead Revisited*.)

Haste (*Deifir*)

Dhá dtrian moille le deifir.
Two thirds of delay is hurrying.
(cf. Less haste; more speed.)

Moillíonn Dia an deifir.
God delays haste.

Ní deabhadh ná é arsa muintir Poimpé.
There is no hurry or the likes, said the people of Pompeii.

Pósadh faoi dhithneas; aithreachas go réidh.
Marry in haste; repent at leisure.

Ní thig luath agus léire le chéile.
Speed and precision do not come together.

Ní thabharfaidh tú do chóta chun na huaighe

Marbh le tae
agus marbh
gan é

Is maith an scáthán súil charad

Is féidir le cat féachaint ar rí

Nuair a thagann an ceann cait go picnic na luch, ní hé chun páirt a ghlacadh sna sacrásaí...

Madra a cheangal le hispíní

Ní stopfaidh dhá chapall déag agus coinnleoirí airgid an titim sneachta in Bialystoc.

Hatred (*Fuath*)

Is measa an fuath ná an feall.
Hatred is worse than treachery.

Maraíonn an fuath an fuathaitheoir.
Hatred kills the hater.

Is fearr an reilig ná gráin shíoraí.
The graveyard is better than lasting hatred.

Má chuireann báid gráin ort, ná tóg teach cois farraige.
If you hate boats, don't build a house by the sea.
(i.e. Don't put yourself in situation that will cause you distress.)

Creimeann an ghráin an croí ina gcothaítear í.
Hatred corrodes the heart in which it's fostered.

An fear a chuireann síolta gránach, bainfidh sé barr míolach fánach.
He who sows seeds of hatred will reap a sparse and miserable harvest.

Health (*Sláinte*)

Is fearr an tsláinte ná na táinte.
Health is better than wealth.

Tabhartas Dé goile folláin.
A healthy appetite is a gift from God.

An té nach leigheasann im ná uisce beatha, níl aon leigheas air.
He whom butter or whiskey do not cure is not curable.

Bíonn intinn fholláin i gcorp folláin.
A healthy body means a healthy mind.

Tosach sláinte codladh.
The beginning of recovery is sleep.

Is í an tsláinte an tseoid is fearr ar domhan.
Health is the greatest treasure in the world.

Heaven (*Neamh*)

Bíonn saibhir agus daibhir le chéile ar neamh.
Both rich and poor are together in heaven.

Bíonn an dá neamh ag an saibhir—ar thalamh agus sna flaithis.
The rich man has two heavens—on the earth and in paradise.

Ní beatha go dul ar neamh.
There is no life until going to heaven.

Is fearr dul ar neamh i gcifleoga ná go hifreann i gcallaí galánta.
It's better to go to heaven in rags than to hell in fine clothes.
(i.e. A clear conscience is better than wealth.)

Bíonn neamh is ifreann i gcroí an duine.
Both heaven and hell are in the human heart.

Bíonn an dá rud sa phósadh – neamh agus ifreann.
Marriage is both heaven and hell.

Hell (*Ifreann*)

Má tá an saibhir ar a bhealach go hifreann, tá an daibhir ann cheana féin.
If the rich man is on his way to hell, the poor man is already there.

Is fearr Aifreann ná ifreann.
Mass is better than hell.

Ifreann sin daoine eile.
Hell is other people.
('*L'enfer, c'est les autres*', Jean-Paul Sartre, 1905—1980)

Níl cuthach ifrinn níos géire ná cuthach mná ar diúltaíodh go maslach di.
Hell hath no fury like a woman scorned.
('Heaven has no rage like love to hatred turned, nor hell a fury like a woman scorned,' *The Mourning Bride* (3,7), William Congreve, 1670—1729)

Tá Ifreann bánaithe agus tá na diabhail go léir anseo.
'Hell is empty and all the devils are here.'
(*The Tempest* (1,2), William Shakespeare, 1564—1616)

Téigh ar neamh ar son aeráide, téigh go hifreann ar son cuideachta.
'Go to heaven for the climate, go to hell for the company.'
(Mark Twain, 1835—1910)

Help (*Cúnamh*)

Is maith an cúnamh lá breá.
It is a good help—a fine day.
(cf. A bright day brightens the spirit.)

Is fearr beagán cuidithe ná mórán trua.
A little help is better than a lot of sympathy.

Is í an lámh a shíntear an lámh a cháintear.
It is the hand that helps that is criticised.

Is giorra cabhair Dé ná an doras.
God's help is closer than the door.

Dá mhéad na bhfear is amhlaidh is fearr.
The more men, the better.
(cf. Many hands make light work.)

Ní raibh gearán riamh faoi iomarca fear meithle.
There has never been a complaint yet about there being too many in a working party.
(i.e. Please feel welcome to join in with the work.
'Meitheal Oibre'—working party.
In rural Ireland, farmers would come together in a '*meitheal*' to help one another at harvest time or when there were pressing jobs that required teamwork. cf. The more, the merrier/Many hands make light work.)

Hindsight (*Iarghaois*)

Is é fál ar an ngort é i ndiaidh na foghla.
It's the fence on the field after the robbery.
(cf. Locking the stable door after the horse has bolted.)

Is fearr féachaint amháin os do chomhair ná dhá fhéachaint siar.
Looking ahead once is better than looking back twice.

Ní gaois iarghaois.
Hindsight is not wisdom.
(cf. Hindsight is no sight.)

Is maith an fáidh deireadh an lae.
The end of the day is a good prophet.

Is maith an scéalaí an aimsir.
Time is a good storyteller.
(cf. Time will tell.)

Tar éis an bháire is saoi gach Gael.
After the game, every Irish person is wise.
(i.e. It's easy to be wise after the event.)

Home *(Baile/Teaghlach)*

Níl aon tinteán mar do thinteán féin.
There is no fireside like your own fireside.

Is glas iad na cnoic i bhfad uainn.
The hills far from home look green.

Is aoibhinn dul ar cuairt agus is fearr i gcónaí bheith i do thigh féin.
It's nice to go on a visit, but there's no better place to be than home.

Bíonn gach fear mar rí ina thigh féin.
Every man is king in his own home.
(cf. An Englishman's home is his castle.)

Is measa scealpóg i méar linbh sa bhaile ná na mílte marbh thar lear.
A splinter in a child's finger at home is worse than a thousand dead abroad.
(i.e. Small problems close by seem more serious than grave tragedies far away.)

Honesty (*Macántacht*)

Is fearr an t-ionracas ná a mhalairt.
Honesty is better than its alternative.
(cf. Honesty is the best policy.)

Téann an fear ionraic chun na croiche.
The honest man goes to the gallows.
(cf. Confess and be hanged!)

Is fearr dom an t-ionracas ach is fearr liom gan é.
Honesty is better for me, but I prefer to be without it.
(cf. Honesty is praised, but starves.)

Tá ionracas os cionn margaidh.
Honesty is above bargaining.
(cf. Honesty cannot be bought or sold.)

Ní insíonn balbhán bréag.
A dumb man tells no lies.

Canann meisce nó fearg fíor.
Drunkenness and anger sing true.

Honour (*Oineach*)

Ní íocann ainm oinigh fiacha.
An honored name doesn't pay the bills.

Ar oilbhéas feirc, ar oineach déirc.
Shameful behaviour has a paunch; honour has to beg.
(i.e. Shameless people live a good life while the honorable must beg.)

Is beag a shalaíonn stocaí bána.
It takes little to sully white socks.
(i.e. A person whose honour is widely acknowledged can easily be smeared by a small transgression that would not be noticed in others.)

An té a chaill a oineach ní bhíonn náire air.
The one who has lost his honour is shameless.

Dílseacht na gceithearnach coille.
Honour amongst thieves.

Is uaisle onóir ná ór.
Honour is finer than gold.

Hope (*Dóchas*)

Dá dhonacht an scéal caithfear dóchas a choinneáil.
However bad the situation, one must keep hoping.
(cf. Hope against hope.)

Tá beocht sa dóchas.
Hope gives life.

An áit a bhfuil beatha tá dóchas ann.
Where there is life, there is hope.

Ní peaca an dóchas.
Hoping is not a sin.
(i.e. There is no harm in hoping.)

Bíonn súil le muir.
The sea offers hope.
(cf. Hope springs eternal. This is part of a longer version: '*Bíonn súil le muir ach ní bhíonn súil leis an uaigh*'—'There is hope from the sea, but no hope from the grave.' i.e. there is no hope of anyone returning from death.)

Hospitality (*Aíocht*)

Is leath den fhéile fáilte chaoin.
Half of hospitality is a warm welcome.

Croith an deannach de do chosa leo!
Have nothing more to do with them!
(Biblical, Luke 9:5: '*Croith an deannach de do chosa!*'—'Shake the dust from off your feet!' i.e. leave a place, person, situation, etc. behind and move on, sometimes quoted to a person who is upset about churlish hospitality.)

Is measa aoi gan fáilte ná iasc lofa sa teach.
An unwelcome guest is worse than a rotten fish in the house.

Cuairt ghearr agus é a dhéanamh go hannamh.
A short visit, and rarely.
(i.e. Never overstay your welcome.)

Den fháilte an fhéile.
Generosity makes the welcome.

Humility (*Umhlaíocht*)

Is maith bheith umhal gan bheith uiríseal.
It is good to be humble, but not servile.

Is féidir le cat féachaint ar rí.
A cat can look at a king.

Bíonn an sárachán lán is an náireachán folamh.
The brazen one is full and the shame-faced empty.

Ná bíodh do theanga faoi do chrios.
Don't let your tongue be under your belt.
(i.e. Speak up! No need to be humble in front of me.)

Is fada ón luaith an bocaire.
The muffin is far from the fireside.
(cf. There's many a slip twixt the cup and the lip.)

Hunger (*Ocras*)

Is maith an t-anlann an t-ocras.
Hunger is the best sauce.

Bíonn fear ocrach feargach.
A hungry man is an angry man.

Ní chuimhníonn an cú gortach ar a choileáin.
The hungry hound doesn't remember its pups.

Císte i mbolg, deoch chun béil agus croí an fhir i do láimh agat.
A cake in the belly, a drink for the lips and the man's heart in your hand.
(cf. The way to a man's heart is through his belly.)

Ní thuigeann sách seang.
The well-fed person does not understand the underfed.

Is fearr leath-bhuilín ná bheith folamh gan arán.
It is better to have half a loaf than to be empty without bread.

Fónann go leor chomh maith le féasta.
Enough serves as well as a feast.

Hypocrisy (*Fimíneacht*)

Ná déan mar a dhéanaim, déan mar adeirim.
Don't do as I do; do as I say.

Go breá cóir chun bealaigh ach fáth na ndeor cois teallaigh.
Fine and pleasant when outside, but cause of tears at home.

Rós ar an tsráid ach driseog sa teach.
A rose on the street but a bramble in the house.
('*driseog*'—bramble, or a prickly, irritable person)

Fearadh aghaidh na hEaglaise go séimh (fearacht Tadhg an dá thaobh).
Let the face of the Church shine mildly (like the hypocrite).
(i.e. The clergy smile at you, but only from the teeth out.)

Ní cheilfear go deo ar an mbith, nuair a bhíonn tú craplaí' istigh.
'One thing you can't hide is when you're crippled inside.'
(John Lennon, 1940—1980)

Is fearr bheith i do pheacaí caointeach ná i do bhéal fimíneach.
It is better to be a weeping sinner than a hypocrite.

Idleness (*Díomhaointeas*)

Is fuath le Dia díomhaointeas.
God hates idleness.

Is fearr pósadh luath ná díomhaointeas mall.
It is better to get married early than slow idleness.
(*'díomhaointeas'*—idleness and being unmarried. A young man or a young woman without a family was considered to be 'idle', which is distinct in Irish from being 'lazy'.)

Is áil le cat a iasc a ithe ach ní háil leis a chrúba a fhliuchadh.
The cat likes its fish, but doesn't like getting its paws wet.
(i.e. Those who wish to achieve something must work while braving the difficulties and inconveniences along the way.)

An fear nach n-oibríonn dó féin oibreoidh sé do dhaoine eile.
He who does not work for himself will work for other people.

Is olc an chearc nach scríobfaidh di féin.
It's a bad hen that won't scratch for itself.

Déanann codladh fada tóin lom.
Protracted sleep makes a bare backside.

Is gnóthach an diabhal i mbothán díomhaoin.
The devil is busy in an idle man's house.
(cf. The devil finds work for idle hands.)

Pocán déirce is cifleoga tuarastal an díomhaointis.
A beggar's bag and tattered rags are the wages of indolence.

Ignorance (*Aineolas*)

Saol an mhadaidh bháin ag leanaí agus dalldramáin.
Children and ignoramuses live a life of bliss.

An rud nach eol duit ní dhéanfaidh dochar duit.
The thing that you don't know cannot harm you.

Níl aon namhaid ach aineolas.
The only enemy is ignorance.

Is mairg don té a thugann droim don fhírinne.
Woe to him who ignores the truth.

Is cara fealltach creideamh caoch.
Blind belief is a false friend.

Dá dhorcha oíche gan solas na ré is duibhe fós ainbhios i ngile an lae.
However dark a moonless night may be, ignorance in brightness of day
is darker by far.

Illness (*Easláinte*)

I dtosach na haicíde is fusa í a leigheas.
It is easier to cure an illness at the start.

Dhá dtrian galair le hoíche.
Sickness is most intense at night.

Galar na gcás galar na hóige; galar an bháis galar na sean.
Youth suffers the illness of perplexity; age the illness of dying.
(i.e. Young people don't know what to do; old people can't do it.)

Níl galar gan leigheas.
There is no illness without a cure.
(i.e. For certain afflictions, the cure is death.)

Níl duine (ann) gan galar éigin air.
Everyone has some affliction.
(cf. Everyone has their own cross to bear.)

Galar gangaideach galar na gcnámh.
Rheumatism/Arthritis is a virulent illness.

Liostachas fada an tseanaois.
Old age is a lingering illness.

Níl aicíd ar bith air ach an aicíd bheag.
He has no illness except the little illness.
('*aicíd bheag*'—a drinking problem)

Imperfection (*Neamhfhoirfeacht*)

Ní bhíonn saoi gan locht.
There isn't a wise man without a fault.

Ní maith le Dia foirfeacht.
God doesn't like perfection.
(i.e. People were superstitious about anything that looked 'perfect', and often would make a deliberate flaw in their own work in order not to seem arrogant in the face of God, who alone could create perfection.)

Is ansa linn laigí beaga ár gcarad.
We love the little weaknesses of our friends.

Bain an tsail as do shúilse féin agus ansin tóg an dúradán as súil do bhráthar.
Remove the beam out of your own eye and then take the speck out of your brother's eye.
(Biblical)

Cá bhfuil rós gan dealg?
Where is there a rose without a thorn?

Inconvenience (*Míchaoithiúlacht*)

Is áil le cat a iasc a ithe ach ní háil leis a chrúba a fhliuchadh.
The cat likes its fish, but doesn't like getting its paws wet.
(i.e. We would like to have things, but do not wish to undergo the inconvenience of acquiring them.)

Deir tú gan dua ach ort do chuireas crua.
You say it's no inconvenience, but I caused you bother.
(cf. There is no convenience without its inconvenience—said to someone who is going out of their way to oblige, while insisting that their giving help has caused them no inconvenience.)

Ní bhíonn an fhírinne i gcónaí caoithiúil.
The truth isn't always convenient.

Ní peaca an bhochtaineacht ach is mór an mhíchaoithiúlacht é.
Poverty is not a sin, but it is great inconvenience.

Inevitability (*Dosheachantacht*)

Ní bhíonn grian gan scáil.
There is no sun without a shadow.
(i.e. Everything has its downside.)

An té a mbeidh sé ina chinniúint aige crochadh, ní bháfar go brách é.
He who is fated to be hanged will never drown.

An uair a bheidh an cupán lán, cuirfidh sé thairis.
When the cup is full it will overflow.

Níl tuile ann nach dtránn.
There is no flood that doesn't ebb.

Is fada an bóthar nach mbíonn casadh ann.
It is a long road that doesn't have a turn in it.

Nuair is crua don chailleach, caithfidh sí rith.
When the hag is hard pressed, she will have to run.

Dá fhad a bhíonn an crúiscín ag iompar uisce, is é a chríoch a bhriseadh.
However long the jug is carrying water, its end is in its breaking.
(i.e. However long something or someone faithfully serves the community, eventually the thing/person comes to its end.)

Inquisitiveness (*Fiosracht*)

Fiosracht na luiche faoi deara a lot—ón eolas a fuair sé saor ón gcat.
The curiosity of the mouse caused his downfall—from the information freely provided by the cat.
(cf. Curiosity killed the cat; information made him fat.)

Duine fiosrach duine eolach.
An inquisitive person is a person who knows things.
(i.e. A certain degree of inquisitiveness is necessary and beneficial.)

Faigheann fiosrach fiúntas.
The inquisitive person finds merit.
(i.e. The inquisitive person will find out and acquire what is worthwhile.)

Slán an caidéiseach!
Bless the inquisitive one!
(i.e. said to someone who shows a healthy and sincere concern in one's personal affairs)

Invitation (*Cuireadh*)

Bíonn fáilte chroíúil roimh chuireadh gan súil.
An unexpected invitation is always greatly appreciated.

Ná cuir do ghob i gcuideachta gan iarraidh.
Never stick your beak into company without an invitation.

Ní cuireadh gan deoch.
It is not an invitation without a drink.

Judgement (*Breith*)

Ná tabhair breith ar an chéad scéal!
Never judge on the first story (you hear)!

Ní ionann i gcónaí cófra agus a lucht.
A cupboard is not always the same as its contents.
(i.e. Don't judge by appearances.)

Is túisce beart ná briathra.
Action is better than words.
(i.e. A person is judged by their actions, not their words.)

Ná tabhair breithiúnas ionas nach dtabharfar breithiúnas ortsa.
Judge not, lest you are judged yourself.
(Biblical, Matthew 7:1. The actual Biblical quotation reads: '*Ná tugaigí breithiúnas ionas nach dtugtar breithiúnas oraibh*'—'Judge not, lest ye be judged.')

Ní breitheamh cothrom an grá.
Love is not an impartial judge.

Justice (*Ceart*)

Níl neart gan ceart.
There is no strength without justice.

Bíonn an ceart ag an neart.
Might is right.

A cheart don té a thuill é.
His due to the one who has earned it.
(cf. Credit where credit is due.)

Ní théann samhail i bhfad.
A comparison does not go far.
(i.e. It is unjust to compare. cf. Comparisons are odious.)

Ní éagóir malairt ionraic.
It is not an injustice an honest exchange.
(cf. Fair exchange is no robbery.)

An ceart roimh an fhéile.
Justice before generosity.

Karma (*Karma*)

Filleann an feall ar an bhfeallaire.
The evil deed returns on the evildoer.

Ní uasal ná íseal ach thuas seal agus thíos seal.
There isn't nobility or ignobility, but up a while and down a while.

Mar a chuirfeas tú bainfidh tú.
As you sow, so shall you reap.

An té nach gcuireann san earrach ní bhainfidh sé san fhómhar.
The one who does not plant in spring will not reap in the autumn.

Ní raibh feall riamh nach bhfillfidh lá éigin.
There hasn't ever been an evil deed that will not one day return (upon the evildoer).

Rotha mór an tsaoil
The big wheel of life.
(The title of the biography of Micí Mac Gabhann (1865—1948), which has now become synonymous with the idea of Samsara and the endless circle of life.)

Kindness (*Cineáltas*)

Níor bhris focal cneasta cnámh riamh.
A kind word never broke a bone.

Níl costas ar chineáltas.
Kindness costs nothing.

Eochair chroí an duine an cineáltas... (...eochair fhlaithis Dé an grá).
The key to the human heart is kindness... (... the key to heaven is love).

Níos luachmhaire ná ór na cineáltais a rinneamar.
More valuable than gold are the kindnesses we have done.

Is fearr buíochas beannachtach ná féirín fuar.
Warm gratitude is better than a cold present.

Má ligtear an gabhar isteach sa séipéal ní stopfaidh sé go haltóir.
If you let a goat into the chapel, he won't stop (until he reaches) the altar.
(cf. Give him an inch and he'll take a mile.)

Kinship (*Gaol*)

Is lom gualainn gan bhráthair.
It is bare a shoulder without a brother.

Is mairg don té a bhíonn gan deartháir.
Woe to him who hasn't got a brother.

Sa bhaile atá an gaol.
It is at home that kinship is.
(i.e. We are loved and cared for best at home.)

An t-olc gan mhaith ar dhroim an choimhthígh.
The bad and worthless on the back of the stranger.
(i.e. If there is trouble at home it is the stranger who is blamed for it.)

Is den chat an t-eireaball.
The tail is part of the cat.
(i.e. Family is one unit, and all members are part of that whole.)

Is tibhe fuil ná uisce.
Blood is thicker than water.

Níor bhris cearc na sicíní a sprochaille riamh.
The hen with chicks never burst its craw.
('*Sprochaille*'—gill, wattle, craw. i.e. feeding its young means that it cannot overindulge.)

Is treise dúchas ná oiliúint.
Nature is stronger than nurture.

Buan fear ina dhúiche féin.
A man lives long in his native place.

Is báúil lucht aon chine.
People of the same stock are friendly.

Aithnítear gaol sa bhearna bhaoil.
Kindred feelings come to the fore in a time of war.
(*'an bhearna bhaoil'*—the gap of danger)

Ní gaol gach Gael.
Not every Gael is a relative.
(i.e. Just because someone shares something in common with you, it does not mean that they are your friend.)

Dá ghaireacht do dhuine a chóta, is giorra dó a léine.
However close to a person their coat, their shirt is closer.
(cf. Charity begins at home/Blood is thicker than water.)

Knowledge (*Eolas*)

Is scéalach siúlach.
The traveller has many stories.
(*'siúlach'*—walker/wanderer)

Fásann crann an eolais in ithir an amhrais.
The tree of knowledge grows in the soil of doubt.

Máthair na suáilce an t-eolas.
Knowledge is the mother of virtue.

Asal faoi ualach leabhar sea léann an chinn ramhair.
A donkey burdened with books is the fat-head's learning.
(i.e. Learning without wisdom is of no use.)

Cuireann an léann iomarcach ar mearú céille thú.
Too much learning drives you mad.
(Based on the Bible, Acts 26:24. This can be used in all tenses depending
on the occasion:
Chuir an léann—'all that learning has driven you mad!'
Cuirfidh an léann—an exhortation to someone to put away their books
and come out to enjoy themselves, cf. All study and no play makes Jack
a dull boy.)

Language/Tongue (*Teanga*)

Tír gan teanga, tír gan anam.
A country without a language is a country without a soul.

Tabharfaidh do theanga chun na Róimhe thú.
Your tongue will bring you to Rome.
(i.e. The clever use of language can achieve great things.)

Is treise peann ná buille/cic sa cheann.
A pen is stronger than a blow/kick to the head.
(cf. The pen is mightier than the sword.)

Focal airgead—ciúine ór!
Speech is silver—silence is gold.

Is marfaí teanga ghéar mná ná claíomh i láimh bithiúnaigh.
A sharp tongue of a woman is more deadly than a sword in the hands of a scoundrel.

Lateness (*Déanaí/Deireanaí*)

Is fearr déanach ná choíche.
Better late than never.

Is minic go raibh déanach ámharach.
It is often late is lucky.

Is minic a bhí cú mall sona.
It's often that a lagging hound was lucky.

Feoil do na seanóirí gan chairb.
Meat for the toothless old-timers.
(i.e. The meat comes too late to be enjoyed. Sometimes the full version
may be used: *Súp do na fearaibh agus feoil do na seanóirí gan chairb*—Men
getting soup and meat for the toothless old-timers.)

Bain spraoi as gach lá agus oíche ó imíonn an bheatha ar nós na gaoithe.
Enjoy every day and every night since life passes by at the speed of light.
(cf. 'Gather ye rosebuds while ye may', from 'To the Virgins, to Make
Much of Time' by Robert Herrick, 1591—1674.)

Go déanach ar maidin, go déanach istoíche,
ní dhéanfaidh sin maitheas ar bith dúinn choíche.
Getting up late and going to bed late,
will never do us any good.

Law (*Dlí*)

Dlí amháin don saibhir agus dlí eile don bhocht.
One law for the rich and another for the poor.

Tugann an dlí smacht ach is mairg don té a bheas ar lorg cirt sa reacht.
Laws keep discipline, but woe to him who seeks for justice in the law.

Beatha ó láimh go béal agus cosa Gallda ar bholg an Ghaeil.
A hand-to-mouth existence and the foreign feet on the belly of the Irish.
(This refers to the Penal Laws—a series of oppressive and unjust laws instigated in Ireland after the Williamite victory of 1691.)

Níl i reachtaibh Gall ach tachtadh Gael.
The laws of the foreigner are only the strangling of the Irish.
(This refers to the Penal Laws—see above.)

Dlíthe ina mbeart nach dtugann aon cheart.
Laws in abundance that don't give us justice.
(An alternative version of this is also used: *Dlíthe ina mbearta nach dtugann dúinn cearta*—Packages of laws that don't give us any rights.)

Laziness (*Leisce/Falsacht*)

Loghann leisce lámh.
Laziness withers dexterity.

Is trom an t-ualach an leisce.
It's a heavy burden laziness.

Tá ualach ná leisce níos troime na ualach na hoibre.
The burden of idleness is heavier than the burden of work.

Déanann codladh fada tóin lom.
Protracted sleep makes a bare backside.

Bíonn ainghníomh, drabhlás agus bruíon ag an diabhal don chladhaire díomhaoin.
The devil has wicked deeds, debauchery and quarrelling to occupy the lazy cad.
(cf. The devil finds work for idle hands.)

Saol caillte saol leisciúil.
A lazy life is a lost/wasted life.

Lending (*Iasacht*)

Airgead ar iasacht airgead imithe.
Money lent is money gone.
(i.e. Forget about any money lent as if it were gone.)

Ná tabhair ar iasacht agus ná tóg ar iasacht.
Don't give a loan or take a loan.
(cf. Neither a borrower nor a lender be.)

Is gnáth sealbh ar an síor-iasacht.
It is usual that a long outstanding loan confers ownership.

Ceileann iasacht bochtaineacht.
Borrowing conceals poverty.

An rud atá tógtha ar iasacht, fág slán leis!
Bid farewell to whatever has been borrowed.

Ní féidir teacht i dtír ar na hiasachtaí.
You cannot survive living on borrowings.
(i.e. All borrowing is only a short-term solution.)

Liberty (*Saoirse*)

Ná tabhair don daoirse diúltamh agus tabharfar saoirse duit.
Don't refuse hardship and you will be given freedom.
(quoted from 'Saoirse' by Seán Ó Ríordáin, 1910—1977)

Níl laistigh den daoirse ach saoirse ón daoirse sin .
There isn't within any hardship but the freedom from that hardship.
(i.e. By facing a difficult task we are liberated. Failing to face up to chal-
lenges will only exacerbate what is troubling us—quoted from 'Saoirse'
by Seán Ó Ríordáin, 1910—1977.)

Is túisce saoirse ná ór.
Freedom is better than gold.

Má tá tú tuirseach den tsaoirse—pós!
If you are tired of freedom—get married!

Ní fios cad í an tsaoirse go daoirse.
We do not know what freedom is until oppressed.

Is seoid í an tsaoirse agus is í an óige an tseoid sin.
Freedom is a jewel and youth is that jewel.

Life (*Beatha/Saol*)

Níl sa saol ach tamall beag.
Life is very short.

Níl sa saol ach gaoth agus toit.
Life is just wind and smoke.

Beatha duine a thoil.
A person's life is his (free) will.
(i.e. Life is only worth living if you have the freedom to choose.)

Tamall beo tamall ag dreo.
Alive a while and withering a while.
(i.e. the transitory nature of life)

Tá beocht sa seanmhadra fós.
There's life in the old dog yet.

Ní beatha go dul ar neamh.
There's no life until we go to heaven.

Is milis an rud an saol.
Life is sweet.

Is ait an mac an saol.
Life is a strange business.

Glac an saol mar a thig sé leat!
Take life as it comes!

Ar scáth a chéile a mhairimid.
We all exist in one another's shadow.

Fiche bliain ag fás, fiche bliain sa rás, agus fiche bliain ag teannadh ar an mbás.
Twenty years a-growing, twenty years in the (rat) race, and twenty years closing in on death.
(Today, on occasions, the *fiche bliain* (twenty years) is being replaced by a slightly more encouraging *tríocha bliain* (thirty years), which perhaps is a tad more optimistic.)

Nuair a rugadh thú, bhí tú ag caoineadh agus bhí lúcháir ar an saol. Caith do shaol sa tslí is go mbeidh an saol ag caoineadh agus lúcháir ortsa nuair a gheobhaidh tú bás.
When you were born, you cried and the world rejoiced. Live your life so that when you die, the world cries and you rejoice.
(Cherokee proverb)

Bailíonn brobh beart.
Many a little makes a mickle.
(A 'mickle' or 'muckle' is a northern English / Scottish term for 'a large amount'.)

Likelihood (*Dealramh*)

Níl ní nach bhfuil indéanta.
Nothing is impossible
(Biblical, Matthew 19:26, taken from the fuller text: '*Níl aon ní nach bhfuil indéanta ag Dia*'—'There is nothing impossible for God.')

Agus tiocfaidh na ba abhaile leo féin.
And the cattle will come home by themselves.
(i.e. There is no likelihood of that! cf. 'When pigs fly.')

Ní bhainfear fuil as tornapa.
Blood will not be got from a turnip.
(cf. It's like trying to get blood from a stone.)

Is annamh go mbítear mar a shíltear.
It is rarely that things happen as one expects.
(cf. *Ní mar a shíltear a bhítear.*)

Bíonn dhá rud dhosheachanta i saol an duine—cánacha agus bás.
There are two unavoidables in anyone's life—taxes and death.

Little (*Beagán*)

Is mór iad na beaganna i dteannta a chéile.
Every little helps.

Ní mór don fhear beag bheith glic.
The small man has to be cunning.

Beagán a rá agus é a rá go maith.
Say a little and say it well.

Bíonn blas ar an mbeagán.
A small amount is appreciated.

Tógann mionchlocha caisleáin mhóra.
Small stones build big castles.

Is é a locht a laghad.
Its only deficiency/fault is that there isn't enough of it.

Is mór an beagán i measc na mbochtán.
A little is a lot to the poor.

Is fearr beag deas ná mór gránna.
Small and nice is better than big and ugly.

Is mór an fad orlach ar shrón.
An inch on a nose is a great length.

Leagfaidh tua beag crann mór.
A small axe will fell a big tree.

Bíonn na hearraí is fearr i mbeairtíní beaga.
The best goods come in small parcels.

Is fearr beagán cuidithe ná mórán trua!
A little help is better than a lot of pity!

Chun obair mhór a chríochnú, ní mór tús beag a chur leis.
To finish great work, it must have a small beginning.

Is beag rud nach faide ná do lámh.
It's the rare thing that is not longer than your hand.
(i.e. Any instrument is better than working with one's bare hands.)

Loiteann aor beag clú mór.
A small satire destroys a great reputation.

Loneliness (*Uaigneas*)

Is fearr an troid ná an t-uaigneas.
Fighting is better than loneliness.

Ní daoirse go huaigneas.
There is no hardship like loneliness.

Is san oíche a dtagann na smaointe is uaigní i gcroí an duine.
The night brings the loneliest thoughts to a human being.

Feonn an t-uaigneas an t-anam.
Loneliness withers the soul.

Nead an mhachnaimh dhoilíosaigh an t-uaigneas.
Loneliness is a nest for desolate thoughts.

Tagann an t-uaigneas leis an tseanaois.
Loneliness accompanies old age.

Loss (*Caill*)

Ní bhíonn imeacht gan chaill.
There is no departure without loss.

Nár chaill an chaill an chailleach.
Didn't the lost thing cause the loss of the hag.
(i.e. Worrying about what has been lost may cause the greater loss of what we are presently enjoying or are about to enjoy. cf. No good crying over spilt milk.)

Is cuid den saol an chaill.
Loss is part of life.

Nuair a thagann an chaill tagann an fhaill.
When the loss arrives, the cliff arrives.
(i.e. Misfortunes never come singly. cf. When it rains, it pours. 'When sorrows come, they come not single spies, but in battalions' *Hamlet*, 4,5.)

Is fearr filleadh as lár an átha ná bá sa tuile.
It is better to return from the middle of the ford than to drown in the flood.
(i.e. It is better to cut your losses.)

Love (*Grá*)

Folaíonn grá gráin.
Love is blind.
(Less frequently quoted is the ending: *...ach feiceann fuath a lán*—... but hatred sees much.)

Níl aon leigheas ar an ghrá ach pósadh.
There is no cure for love except marriage.

Capall na beatha an grá.
The horse of life is love.
(cf. Love makes the world go round.)

Maireann lá go ruaig ach maireann an grá go huaigh.
A day lasts until it's chased away, but love lasts until the grave.

Ceileann searc ainimh is locht.
Love hides defect and fault.
(cf. Love is blind.)

Galar an grá nach leigheasann luibheanna.
No known herb cures love.

Níl lia ná leigheas ar an ghrá.
There is no physician or cure for love.

Fearg is fuath naimhde an fhíorghrá.
Anger and hatred are the enemies of true love.

Is dall an grá baoth.
Self-love is blind.

Is doiligh éalú ó gheasa an ghrá.
It's hard to escape from the bonds of love.

Fuaraíonn grá go grod.
Love cools quickly.

Ní dheachaigh fear meata chun bantiarna.
The cowardly man did not go to the lady.
(cf. Faint heart never won fair lady.)

Ní breitheamh cothrom an grá.
Love is not an impartial judge.

Ní beatha (é) gan ghrá.
There is no life without love.

Grá inneall na beatha agus tiománaí an tsaoil.
Love is the engine of life and it drives the world.

Luck (*Ádh*)

An té a bhíonn thíos buailtear cloch faoi, is an té a bhíonn thuas óltar deoch air.
The one who is down is kicked underfoot, and the one that is up is toasted.
(i.e. People are fickle in their loyalties and praise.)

Bíonn an mí-ádh féin ar gach duine uair éigin.
Everyone gets their share of bad luck sometime.

Is caol mar a ritheann sruth an áidh ach is ina thuillte móra a thagann an mí-ádh.
The stream of luck/good fortune flows narrowly, but misfortune comes in floods.

Is fearr an t-ádh maith ná éirí go moch.
Good fortune is better than getting up early.

Is fearr bheith sona ná críonna.
It is better to be lucky than wise.

Más fada ag teacht an t-ádh, tagann sé faoi dheireadh.
Luck may be slow to come, but it comes eventually.

An té a mbíonn an t-ádh ar maidin air bíonn sé air maidin is tráthnóna.
The one who is lucky in the morning is lucky in the morning and the afternoon.
(The opposite is also frequently used: *An té a bhfuil an mí-ádh ar maidin air, bíonn sé air maidin is tráthnóna*—The one who is unlucky in the morning will be unlucky in the morning and the afternoon.)

Fanann fear sona séan.
The lucky man waits for the auspicious moment.

Is minic go raibh déanach ámharach.
It is often late is lucky.

Is minic a bhí cú mall sona.
It's often that a lagging hound was lucky.

Bíonn an t-ádh ar amadáin.
Fools have luck.

Ádh an tosaitheora!
Beginner's luck!

Dá dhéine a bhítear ag obair, is é is mó an t-ádh.
The harder one works, the more the luck.
(cf. 'The harder I work, the luckier I seem to get', attributed to Thomas Jefferson, 1743—1826)

Manners (*Béasa*)

Is fearr dea-bhéas ná dea-ainm.
Good manners are better than a good name.

Is fearr béasa ná breáthacht.
Good manners are better than good looks.

Ní lia tír ná nós.
Every country has its own customs.

Ná déan nós agus ná bris nós!
Don't make or break a tradition. Do as everyone else does.
(a call to conformity)

Is fearr dea-bhéasa ná éadaí galánta.
Good manners are better than fine attire.

Nuair a bhíonn tú ar an oileán, glac le nósanna an oileáin.
When you are on the island, accept the customs of the island.
(cf. When in Rome, do as the Romans do.)

Marriage (*Pósadh/Cleamhnas*)

Iarr ar bhean uair nó dhó agus mura dtagann lig go deo!
Ask a woman once or twice to marry you—if she refuses, let her be forever!

Pós bean oileáin agus pósfaidh tú an t-oileán ar fad.
Marry an island woman and you marry the whole island.

An té nach bpósann níl ach uaigneas dlite dósan.
He who does not marry will be lonely.

Mairg nach ndéanann comhairle dea-mhná.
Woe to him who does not have the counsel of a good wife.

(toast) *Sliocht sleachta ar shliocht bhur sleachta!*
May you have children and your children have children!

(proposal of marriage) *An luífeása le mo mhuintirse?*
Would you like to lie (i.e. be buried) with my people?

An té a phósann an t-airgead, pósfaidh sé óinseach. Imeoidh an t-airgead agus fanfaidh an t-óinseach.
The one who marries money gets a fool for a wife. The money will go but the fool will remain.

Message (*Teachtaireacht*)

Ná cuir dailtín le teachtaireacht!
Don't send a child with a message!

Teachtaire an drochscéil (is ea) teachtaire i mbaol.
A messanger with bad news is a messanger in danger.

Ná maraigh an teachtaire.
Don't kill the messenger.

Dea-scéala gan aon scéala!
No news is good news.

Scéal ar bith atá gránna á scaipeadh go dána.
Any unpleasant news spreads boldly.
(cf. Bad news travels fast.)

Is í an phóg teachtaire an ghrá.
A kiss is the messenger of love.

Miserliness
(*Sprionlaitheacht/Gortaíl*)

Ní fhaigheann lámh iata ach dorn dúnta.
A closed hand only gets a shut fist.

Féile ghortacháin i dteach an doichill!
The niggard's generosity in a churlish house!
(Said about a mean and miserable reception given to guests in a house celebrating some event.)

An té is mó a osclaíonn a bhéal is lú a osclaíonn a sparán.
The one who opens his mouth the most opens his purse the least.

Béal eidhneáin croí cuilinn.
Mouth of ivy, heart of holly.
(i.e. Somebody who has a prickly way of speaking, but nonetheless has 'sacred' intentions.)

Bíonn an sprionlóir i ngátar i gcónaí.
The miser is always in need.

Mac an ghortacháin a dhéanann flaisc.
The son of the miser is (usually) a spendthrift.

Moderation (*Measarthacht*)

An mheasarthacht i ngach rud.
Moderation in all things.

Is fusa gabháil lár báire.
It's easier to take the middle way.

An mheasarthacht fiú sa mheasarthacht.
Moderation even in moderation.

Daingneacht tuarastail a chothaíonn an mheasarthacht.
Security of salary fosters mediocrity.

Is í an iomaíocht namhaid na measarthachta.
Competition is the foe of mediocrity.

Money (*Airgead*)

Ní bhíonn airgead amadáin i bhfad ina phóca.
The money of a fool isn't long in his pocket.

Is fearr cara sa chúirt ná céad punt sa phóca.
A friend in court is better than a hundred pounds in your pocket.

Is fearr réal inniu ná scilling amárach.
A sixpence today is better than a shilling tomorrow.

Ní hé an fear a thuilleann is mó a fhaigheann is mó.
It isn't the person who deserves the most, earns the most.

Cuireann an t-airgead an domhan ag damhsa.
Money gets the world dancing.
(cf. Money makes the world go round.)

Ní féidir a grá a cheannach le hór.
You cannot buy love with gold.
(cf. Money can't buy you love.)

Music (*Ceol*)

Nuair a stadann an ceol stopann an rince.
When the music ceases, the dancing stops.

Fáilte, féile agus fleá roimh pháiste agus cheoltóir breá.
Welcome, generosity and feasting on the birth of a child and the arrival of a good musician.

Spléachadh isteach i bhflaithis Dé an ceol.
Music is a glimpse of heaven.

Is minic gur fearr ceol ná feoil.
It is often that music is better than meat.

Ní bhíonn meas ar phíobaire an aon phoirt.
There isn't respect for the piper of the one tune.

Bia don chorp, deoch don bheol, comhrá, damhsa, agus ceol.
Food for the body, drink for the lips, chat, dancing and music.
(i.e. The things considered to be the constituents of a good life.)

Nature (*Nádúr/Dúchas*)

Is treise dúchas ná oiliúint.
Nature is stronger than nurture.

Cad a dhéanfaidh mac an chait ach luch a mharú.
What will the son of a cat do but kill a mouse?

Ní athróidh foghlaim an nádúr cam.
A crooked nature cannot be corrected by learning.

Ní féidir nádúr ná grá a cheilt.
Neither love nor nature can be hidden.

Nádúr an naoimh bheith foighneach.
It is a saint's nature to be patient.

Necessity/Need (*Riachtanas*)

Múineann gá seift.
Necessity is the mother of invention.

Ní thuigeann sách seang.
The one with plenty does not understand the one in need.

Ní aithníonn gátar aon dlí.
Necessity does not recognise any law.

An rud is gá gheofar é ó Dhia lá.
The thing that is necessary will be received from God one day.

Ó láimh go béal an trá ar fad ó ní féidir teacht i dtír gan bhád.
A subsistence existence along the beach, since to survive you need a boat.
(i.e. A subsistence diet can be achieved by foraging along the seashore, but if you want any decent standard of living a boat is needed. In other words, any activity that will bring a decent profit will require having the correct tools for the job.)

Neighbours (*Comharsana*)

Ní cara comharsa agus ná déan namhaid de.
A neighbour isn't a friend, and don't make him an enemy.

Tabhair do chuid do do chomharsana is bí féin i d'óinseach!
Give what is yours to your neighbour and be a fool yourself!

Ní bhíonn a fhios ag fear an tí thall cad é mar atá fear an tí abhus.
One neighbour doesn't know how it is for the other.
(i.e. No one knows how the other lives.)

Gráigh do chomharsa mar tú féin.
Love your neighbour as yourself.
(Biblical)

Bíonn sonas agus donas ina gcomharsana béil dorais.
Happiness and woe are next-door neighbours.

Bíonn uibheacha i ndíon na gcomharsan i gcónaí níos blasta.
The eggs in the neighbours' roof are always tastier.
(In rural Ireland, hens would lay their eggs in the thatched roofs. In semi-detached cottages, squabbles would occur between neighbours as to whose side of the roof the eggs had been laid on.)

Is fearr comharsa mhaith béil dorais ná gaolta i bhfad ó bhaile.
A good neighbor next door is better than relations far away.

Roinn an síol maith le do chomharsa agus bainfidh tú fómhar maith.
Share the good seed with your neighbour and you will reap a good harvest.
(i.e. If your neighbour sows poor-quality seeds, then when the wind blows, these seeds will end up in your field, so in order to avoid this happening the proverb suggests sharing good seeds. The message is that generosity is always the best way to live because generosity yields the best harvests.)

Fál maith a dhéanas comharsana maithe.
'Good fences make good neighbours' (Robert Frost).
(Although this line from 'Mending Wall' is often quoted, Frost did not believe that good fences make good neighbours—the point of the poem is quite the reverse!

Irish people, however, were, and indeed still are, obsessed by the zealous ownership of their land. There was a tradition that land-boundaries were demarcated by the placing of stones by the farmer. Nonetheless, unscrupulous neighbours would move these stones during the night and then squabbling would break out over where the boundary was. This proverb is historic in its origins and its use. What it means today is that people should be clearly aware of where the boundaries lie between them and other people in order to avoid unneeded conflict. Interestingly, 'good' in the Irish psyche is frequently attached to the amount of property or land a person owns. As there is only so much land to go around, the more land my neighbour has, the less there is for me; the more 'good' my neighbour has the less 'good' I can have. It is from this kind of mindset that the infamous concept of Irish 'begrudgery' arises.)

News (*Nuacht/Scéala*)

Easpa scéala dea-scéala.
A lack of news is good news.

Is maith scéal gan (aon) drochscéal.
No bad news is good news.

Bíonn an drochscéal i gcónaí ar cosa in airde.
Bad news is always on the gallop.
(cf. Bad news travels fast.)

Tarraingíonn scéal scéal eile.
One story attracts another story.

Bíonn an dea-scéal ar leathchois ach bíonn an droch-scéal ar chapall rása.
Good news is lame but bad news rides on a racehorse.

Téigh thar lear agus beidh gach scéal agat ar a bhfuil ag tarlú sa bhaile.
Go abroad and you will know about everything that is happening at home.
(i.e. If you want to know what is happening around your home/ home town, go far away and you will be kept informed about everything.)

Night (*Oíche*)

Chomh fhad an oíche tig an lá.
However long the night, the day will come.

Oíche aerach agus maidin bhrónach.
A fun night and a bum/sad morning.

Dubhobair choíche a dhéantar faoi scáth na hoíche.
The evil work is always is done under the cover of night.

Is ionann saol gan foghlaim agus bheith ag siúl san oíche (gan solas).
A life without an education is like walking in the night (without a light).

Lá—aimsir na bhfear, oíche—aimsir na mban.
The day belongs to men, the night to women.
(This proverb probably dates back to Pagan Ireland when women were considered to be more in touch with magic and the spirits of the shadow world. If men were seen as beings of physical strength, women were considered more as spiritual beings with powers from the unseen world that were identified with darkness and the night.)

Occupation (*Ceird*)

Is namhaid ceird gan chleachtadh.
An unpractised trade becomes an enemy.

Leath na ceirde an uirlis.
Half the trade is the tool.

Tagann máistreacht le cleachtadh.
Mastery comes with practice

Is fearr ceird mhaith ná pota óir.
A good trade is better than a pot of gold.

An té a bhfuil ceird aige ní bhíonn ceangal ná cuibhreach air.
The person who has a trade has no binding or fetter on him.

Iascaire i siopa táilliúra.
A fisherman in a tailor's shop.
(i.e. about a person who is out of place and looks awkward)

Is maith an t-iascaire an té atá ar an talamh.
He is a good fisherman the one who is on (dry) land.
(cf. The hurler on the ditch is always the best.)

Lámh thréan ar an ghabha, súil ghrinn ar an sealgaire.
The smith has a strong arm, the hunter a sharp eye.
(i.e. Each occupation requires its own skills and strengths.)

Firéad ag fiagaí agus leabhair ag an sagart.
A huntsman has his ferret and the priest his books.
(i.e. Every occupation has its own requirements.)

Bean an ghréasaí gan bhróga.
The wife of the cobbler without shoes.

Bíonn cleasa le foghlaim i ngach ceird.
There are tricks to be learnt in every trade.

Tógann gadaí fiú na blianta fada chun máistreacht a fháil ar a cheird.
Even a thief takes many years to master his trade.

Duine gan cheird—duine gan todhchaí.
A person without a trade is a person without a future.

Ceileann lámh oilte dua na hoibre.
A skilled hand conceals the difficulty of the work.
(i.e. Someone who is skilled makes what they do look easy. cf. The art
that hides the art.')

Opportunity (*Deis/Uain*)

Is olc an ghaoth nach séideann do dhuine éigin.
It's an evil wind that doesn't blow good for someone.

Buail an t-iarann fad is atá sé te.
Strike the iron while it is hot.

Sábháil an fómhar fad is a bhíonn an ghrian thuas.
Save the harvest while the sun is up.
(cf. Make hay while the sun shines.)

Is é an ceannaí moch a dhéanann an margadh.
It is the early merchant who clinches the deal.

Tá dhá lá san earrach níos fearr ná deich lá san fhómhar.
Two days in the spring are better than ten days in autumn.

An té nach gcuireann san earrach ní bhaineann sé san fhómhar.
The one who doesn't sow in the spring will not reap in the autumn.

Ní fhanann uain ná taoide le haon duine.
Opportunity or the tide wait for no person.

Éist le fuaim na habhann agus gheobhaidh tú breac.
Listen to the sound of the stream and you will get a trout.

Is fearr an mhaith atá ná an dá mhaith dá fheabhas nár tháinig fós agus nach dtiocfaidh choíche.
One good thing now is better than the two good things, however excellent, that have not and may never come.
(i.e. Do not jeopardise the good that is available now for a perfection that most probably cannot be achieved. cf. The best is the enemy of the good.)

Is fearr amhail ná dóigh.
Thus is better than maybe.

Deis a dhéanann deis.
One opportunity leads to another.

Spéirbhean le cúl a cinn maol is ea an seans sciobtha den sonas sa saol.
Opportunity is fleeting, like a fair maiden without hair on the back of her head.
(i.e. In medieval times, opportunity was depicted as a beautiful maiden with long, flowing hair. As she passed by, you could grab her by the hair, but as soon as she had passed, it was no longer possible because the back of her head was completely bald and there was nothing to hold on to.)

Fásann líon na ndeiseanna de réir mar thapaítear iad.
Opportunities multiply as they are seized.
(Sun Tzu, 544—496 BC)

Patience (*Foighne*)

Faigheann foighne fortacht.
All comes to him who waits.

Foighne leigheas seanghalair.
Patience is the best treatment for an old complaint.

Is suáilce an fhoighne nach dtugann náire.
Patience is a virtue that brings no shame.

Is ceirín do gach lot an fhoighne.
Patience is the poultice for every wound.

Beart gan leigheas foighne is fearr air.
What can't be cured must be endured.

Is den tsuáilce an fhoighne.
Patience is a virtue.

Dá fhad an oíche tig an lá.
However long the night, the day will come.

Níl tuile dá mhéad nach dtránn.
No matter how great the flood, it will subside.

I ndiaidh a chéile a tógadh na caisleáin.
By degrees, the castles were built.
(cf. Rome wasn't built in a day.)

Tig maith mór as moill bheag.
Often great good comes from a short delay.

Déanann foighne foirfeacht.
Patience brings perfection.

Fainic fearg fhear na foighne!
Beware of the anger of a patient man!
(i.e. when patient people finally become angry, their temper is dangerous)

Is fada an bóthar nach mbíonn casadh ann.
It is a long road that has no turn in it.
(i.e. Have patience and the situation will eventually change.)

Is fada le fear na fionraí.
It is long for the waiting man.
(cf. A watched pot never boils.)

Payment (*Íocaíocht*)

Ní íoctar as an mbuille ná mbuailtear.
A blow not given isn't paid for.
(i.e. One does not pay the price for actions left undone.)

Binneas fíon' inniu tinneas cinn amárach.
The sweetness of wine today—the headache tomorrow.

Craic is teaspach dí faic agus easpa ina dhiaidh!
Fun out of a bottle with nothing but want to follow!

Is fiú a thuarastal an t-oibrí.
The labourer is worthy of his wages/hire.
(Biblical)

Is é an bás tuarastal an pheaca.
Death is the wages of sin.
(Biblical)

Daingneacht tuarastail a chothaíonn an mheasarthacht.
Security of salary fosters mediocrity.

Peace (*Síocháin/Suaimhneas*)

Is fearr síocháin ná síorchogadh.
Peace is better than continuous war.
(i.e. Perhaps a reasonable compromise is better than endless quarrelling.)

Is fearr an chaint a thagann as an tsíocháin.
Talk that brings peace is best.

Seacht só de gach sórt ag fear na síochána.
A man of peace has plenty of everything.

Síocháin fhial a thugann saol na bhfuíoll.
A seemly/proper peace brings prosperity.

Tugann aois laoch dána chun síochána.
Age pacifies the brave warrior.

Is é an suaimhneas is fearr.
It is better to do things quietly.
(i.e. Peaceful means wherever possible are more advantageous.)

Is treise peann ná buille/cic sa cheann
The pen is stronger than a blow/kick to the head.
(cf. The pen is mightier than the sword.)

Is measa aoir fút ná saighead tríd an aer ch'út.
It is worse to have a satire written about you than to have an arrow
coming through the air towards you.

People (*Daoine*)

People in general (*Daoine i gcoitinne*)

Castar na daoine ar a chéile!
People meet one another!
(i.e. It's a small world. The full version goes: *Castar na daoine ar a chéile ach ní chastar na cnoic ná na sléibhte*—People meet one another, but hills and the mountains do not. This implies that when people travel they will meet people they haven't seen for years or in unusual parts of the world.)

Is minic gur fearr beirt ná triúr.
Often two people is better than three.
(cf. Two's company; three's a crowd.)

Giorraíonn beirt bóthar.
Two shorten the road.
(i.e. When people do things together it's more fun.)

Glac an saol mar a thig sé leat.
Take life as your find it.
('*saol*'—life, people; i.e. Take people as you find them.)

Women (*mná*)

Níl rud níos géire ná teanga mná.
There is nothing sharper than a woman's tongue.

An áit a mbíonn mná bíonn caint.
Wherever there are women there is talk.

Deacair taobh a thabhairt leis na mná.
It is difficult to trust a woman.

Tá trí shaghas ban atá ann: bean chomh mí-náireach le muc, bean chomh crosta le cearc agus bean chomh mín leis an uan.
There are three kinds of women: a woman as shameless as a pig, a woman as contrary as a hen, and a woman as gentle as a lamb.

Triúr fear go dteipeann orthu mná a thuiscint: fir óga, fir aosta agus fir mheánaosta.
Three kinds of men who fail to understand women: young men, old men and middle-aged men.

Old people (*Seandaoine*)

Ná codail oíche i dteach a bhfuil seanduine pósta le bean óg.
Don't spend the night in the house where an old man is married to a young woman.

Tagann an ghaois le haois.
Wisdom comes with old age.

Ní sonas seanaois ní bainis bás.
Old age isn't happiness; death isn't a wedding.

Ní féidir ceann críonna a chur ar ghualainn óig.
It is not possible to put a wise head on a young shoulder.

Dá ndéanfadh duine óg dá bhféadfadh duine críonna.
If a young person would, if an old person could.

Ní baois go seanaois.
There isn't (real) foolishness until old age.
(i.e. Old people have nothing to lose and therefore can act foolishly.)

Young people and children
(*Daoine óga agus páistí*)

Mol an óige agus tiocfaidh sí.
Praise youth and it will prosper.

Is minic mac maith ag fear na díchéille.
It is often a foolish man has a good son.

Fuathaíonn leanbh loiscthe tine.
A burnt child abhors fire.

Ní thagann an óige faoi dhó choíche.
Youth only comes once.

Is buaine an buinneán maoith ná crann brománta.
A tender twig is stronger than a stubborn tree.
(i.e. Youth is more flexible and therefore more capable of adapting.)

An rud a chí an leanbh ní an leanbh.
The thing that a child sees, he does.
(*a chí—a fheiceann; a ní—a dhéanann*)

Is minic a rinne bromach gioblach capall cumasach.
It is often that a ragged colt makes a powerful horse.
(i.e. Unpromising situations and people can sometimes blossom into something/someone truly wonderful.)

Is éigean don leanbh lámhacán roimh shiúl.
A child has to crawl before it walks.

Gach dailtín mar a oiltear.
Every pup as it is trained.
(i.e. Often said to excuse bad behaviour in the very young, placing the blame upon the parents.)

Páistí ár saol, ár saibhreas, agus ár seanaois.
Children are our life, our wealth and old age.
(i.e. Old people depend upon children in their old age.)

Ní sonas go saolaítear clann.
The greatest joy is the birth of (our) children.
(The continuation is often omitted but understood: *agus ní thuigtear brón go dtí é!*—and sorrow is not understood until then.)

Teach gan sliocht—teach bocht.
A house without progeny is a poor dwelling.

Ná caith an cliabhán amach agus an leanbán ann.
Don't throw the crib out with the baby.
(cf. Don't throw the baby out with the bathwater.)

Fágadh mise leis an malartán.
I was left with the changeling.
(cf. 'I was left holding the baby.' In ancient Ireland people believed that the fairies came and replaced the real baby with a '*malartán*' or 'changeling'. The changeling would scream and cry all the time, and so to be left 'holding the changeling' is to be left on your own to sort out a dreadful/impossible situation. Cf. to 'carry the can'.)

Perception (*Tuiscint*)

Is olc an ghaoth nach séideann do dhuine éigin.
It's an evil wind that doesn't blow good for someone.

Ní mar a shíltear a bhítear.
It is never as you imagine.

Ní heolas go haontíos.
You never know someone until you live with them.

Ocht radharc—ocht gcuimhne.
Eight observations—eight recollections

An rud is annamh is iontach.
The thing that is rare is wonderful.

Cruthú na putóige a hithe.
The proof of the pudding is in the eating.

Más den síoda féin an gúna, ní éasca é a bhaint de Úna.
Even if the dress is made of silk itself, it will not be easy to remove it
from Úna.
(Although something may superficially be seen as accessible or easy to
do, often such perceptions are a wholly incorrect simplification of hidden
complexities.)

Perseverance (*Buanseasmhacht*)

Faigheann rún daingean an chraobh.
The steadfast purpose wins the laurels.
(cf. Perseverance wins the game.)

I ndiaidh a chéile a tógadh na caisleáin.
By degrees, the castles were built.

Ó loisceadh an choinneal loisc an t-orlach.
Since the candle is burnt, burn the inch.
(i.e. Once you have started something, finish it. The 'inch' refers to the final inch of the candle. cf. In for a penny, in for a pound!)

Is breá le Dia tiarálaí buan.
God likes a slogger.
(cf. If at first you don't succeed, try, try again.)

Planning (*Pleanáil*)

Cuir luath agus bain luath!
Sow early and reap early!

Féach sula léime tú
Look before you leap!

Ná cuir do chuid uibheacha ina aon chiseán amháin.
Don't put all your eggs into one basket.

Is fearr breathnú romhat ná dhá bhreathnú i do dhiaidh.
One look in front of you is better than two looks behind you.

Is minic a bhain duine slat a bhuailfeadh é féin.
It is often a person has cut a rod to beat himself.

An té nach gcuirfidh greim cuirfidh sé dhá ghreim.
At stitch in time saves nine.

Beatha gan smaointiú beatha amú.
Life without thinking is a worthless life.

Pollution (*Truailliú*)

Ná truailligh do thairseach féin.
Don't pollute your own doorstep.
(i.e. Don't do bad things in your own neigbourhood.)

Is olc an t-éan a shalaíonn a nead féin.
It is a bad bird that fouls its own nest.

Is leithne an bhualtrach den tsatailt uirthi.
The cow-dung is wider from stamping on it.
(i.e. Don't gossip about bad news or evil happenings as it only helps to exacerbate the situation.)

Is cineál den truailliú an t-aineolas.
Ignorance is a form of pollution.

Seachnaímis truailliú is bás—caomhnaímis an comhshaol glas!
Let's avoid pollution and death—let's protect the green environment!
(Green Party slogan)

Níl romhainn ach baol is bás mura bhfanann an comhshaol glas!
There is only danger and death ahead if the environment doesn't remain green.
(Green Party Slogan)

Possession (*Seilbh*)

Is minic gur fearr liom ná agam.
It is often that I would prefer (something) to belong to me than to have it.
(cf. Possession is nine points of the law. This is a play on the prepositions with pronominal endings '*le*' and '*ag*': '*liom*' signifies ownership whereas '*agam*' describes possession.)

Saibhir an té i seilbh tí, daibhir an té ar cíos.
The one who owns a house is rich; he who rents is poor.

Má thugaim uaim a bhfuil agam agus mura bhfuil grá i mo chroí, ní tairbhe ar bith dom é.
If I give away all I have but have no love in my heart, it is of no benefit to me.
(Adapted saying from the Bible, 1 Corinthians 13:3: Giving away possessions is not a virtue in itself.)

Saol gairid agus iasacht ghairid gach rud againn ar linn.
It is a short life and a short loan of everything that belongs to us.
(i.e. This life is short and we have only a loan of all that we possess.)

Is fearr breac sa láimh ná bradán sa linn.
A trout in the hand is worth a salmon in the pool.

Meum, tuum, suum faoi deara caill is gruaim.
Mine, thine, his/hers are the cause of loss and sorrow.
(From Latin: *meum*—mine, *tuum*—thine, *suum*—his/hers/its)

Bíodh rud agat féin nó bí ina éagmais.
Have something yourself or do without it.

Poverty (*Bochtaineacht*)

Ní minic a bhíos bocht greannmhar.
A poor man's jokes are seldom appreciated.

Ní náire an bhochtaineacht.
Poverty is not shame.

Cré na coiriúlachta an bhochtaineacht.
The clay of crime is poverty.

Is coim cábán an bhoicht.
The poor man's cabin is a covering/shelter.
('*coim*'—shelter, covering)

Is fuath an feic fear fiúntach folamh.
It is a hateful thing to see a worthy man down in his fortunes.

Téann an grá an fhuinneog amach nuair a bhuaileann an gátar isteach.
Love goes out the window when poverty enters.

Milleann an bhochtaineacht coinníoll.
Poverty destroys a pledge.

Cabhair an bhochtáin béal na huaighe.
The poor man's help is the mouth of the grave.

Ní sheasann sac folamh.
An empty sack doesn't stand.

Ní baol don bhacach an gadaí.
The tramp need not fear the thief.

Ní fiú aoibh an tsó don té nach mblaisfeadh riamh anró dá ré.
The smile of prosperity is never deserved by whomever is not willing to suffer hardship in his time.

Is ait le daoine dealbha bláthach.
Buttermilk makes poor people happy.
(*'ait'*—happy)

Gach bocht le muir gach saibhir le sliabh.
Every poor man to the sea; every rich man to the mountain.

Bochtaineacht a dhéanann cumha.
Poverty brings sorrow.

Praise (*Moladh*)

Mol an óige agus tiocfaidh sí.
Praise youth and it will prosper.

Ná mol agus ná dímhol gort nó go rachaidh mí mheáin an tsamhraidh thart.
Do not praise or dispraise a field until the month of June is over.

Ná mol agus ná cáin tú féin!
Never praise or criticise yourself!

Bia anama an linbh moladh cuí.
Appropriate praise is food for a child's spirit.
(i.e. Children need praise and encouragement to achieve their true potential.)

Moladh gach duine an t-ádh mar a gheobhaidh.
Let each person praise the ford as he finds it.

Mol an lá um thráthnóna.
Praise the day in the afternoon.

Molann obair an fear.
Work praises the man.

Moladh luath agus cáineadh mall.
Let praise be early and criticism late.

Molann an gníomh é féin.
The deed praises itself.
(cf. Actions speak louder than words.)

Prayer (*Paidir*)

Abair paidir agus fág faoi Dhia é!
Say a prayer and let God do the rest.

Ní bán buí agus ní paidir guí.
White is not yellow and prayer is not a wish(-list).

Is minic paidrín fada ag rógaire.
It is often that a rogue has a long prayer.

Teaghlach i bpaidir le chéile a bhéas i staidéar le chéile!
A family that prays together stays together!
('*Staidéar*'—in Munster Irish means staying/lodging', cf. '*i nDún Chaoin go mbíodh staidéar ar an mbuachaill*' (*An tOileánach*, p. 184.) A humorous reply to this saying is: *Teaghlach ag taoscadh le chéile a chaillfear go héasca le chéile!*—A family that drinks together sinks together!)

Tá cumhacht sa phaidir.
There is power in prayer.

'*Más mian leis na déithe tú a smachtú, tosaíonn siad le do thoil a reachtú.*'
'If the gods want to punish you, they start by answering your prayers.'
(Oscar Wilde)

Procrastination (*Moilliú*)

Ná cuir gnó an lae inniu go dtí amárach.
Don't put off till tomorrow what you can do today.

Déanann gach moch a ghnó.
The early riser gets through his business.

An rud a théann i bhfad téann sé i bhfuaire.
The thing that goes on (too) long grows cold.
(cf. Procrastination is the thief of time.)

Éasca nóin ná maidin.
Afternoon is easier than morning.

Bíonn fear deireanach díobhálach.
A man who is wont to be late is at a loss.
(This saying can be understood in a few ways: (i) The man who is (often) late is courting trouble; (ii) The man who is (often) late brings harm (to others); (iii) The man who is (often) late will make no good.)

Déanann codladh fada tóin lom.
Long sleeping makes for a bare bum.
(i.e. Poverty is the result of laziness.)

Ná cuir an mhaith ar cairde.
Don't postpone a good deed.

Ní fhanann trá le fear mall.
The ebb-tide waits for no man.
(i.e. Do not procrastinate.)

Profit (*Brabús*)

Cad é an tairbhe é do dhuine seilbh a fháil ar an domhan ar fad, agus seilbh a anam féin a chailleadh?
What shall it profit a man if he shall gain the whole world and lose his own soul?
(Biblical)

Is minic a cheaptar bradán le cuileog.
A salmon is often caught by a fly.

Ní chruinníonn cloch reatha caonach.
A rolling stone gathers no moss.

Is fearr slat de chuntar ná gabháltas talún.
A yard of the counter is worth more than a holding of land.
(i.e. The farmer's life is far harder one than the life of a business person.)

Bíonn an mhil milis ach bíonn an bheach cealgach.
The honey is sweet but the bee stings.
(i.e. You have to work hard to make a sweet profit.)

An té a bhfuil bó aige, is fusa dó lao a bheith aige.
It is easy for him who has a cow to have a calf.

233

Property (*Maoin/Úinéireacht*)

Is minic gur fearr liom ná agam.
It is often that I would prefer (something) to belong
to me than to have it.
(cf. Possession is nine points of the law.)

Ná fág fuíoll an táilliúra i do dhiaidh.
Don't leave the tailor's remnant after you.
(i.e. Take all the cloth you paid for before leaving.)

Is éasca scaipeadh ná bailiú.
It is easier to disperse (property, wealth etc.) than to acquire.

Sáraíonn eagna agus léann tailte, saibhreas agus céim.
Wit and learning beat property, riches and position.
('*tailte*'—lands)

Is fearr go mór id' chábán féin scallta ná i bpálás galánta uasail Ghallda.
It's better by far in your own paltry cabin than in the elegant palace of a
foreign nobleman.

Is fada an ród gan maoin ná dídean.
It's a long road without property or shelter.

Amharc ar neamh, an choinneal i bhfuinneog
do bhotháin féin d'éis aistir fhada.
It is a view of heaven, the candle in the window
of your own house after a long journey.

Proverbs (*Seanfhocail*)

Ní sháraítear na seanfhocail.
Proverbs cannot be surpassed.

Má thréigtear an seanfhocal, ní bhréagnaítear é.
If the proverb is abandoned, it is (never) refuted.

Oidhreacht na smaointe i seanfhocail sinsear.
A heritage of thoughts is to be found in the proverbs of (our) ancestors.

Is ionann seanfhocal agus cogar gaoise ónár sinsir.
A proverb is like a whisper from our ancestors.

Is annamh nach bhfaigheann rógaire seanfhocal cuí.
It is rare that a rogue cannot find an appropriate proverb.
(i.e. Watch out for confidence tricksters who can smooth-talk a person by their readiness of speech.)

Recognition (*Aithne*)

Aithníonn ciaróg ciaróg eile.
One beetle recognises another.

Éanlaith na heite céanna in éineacht ag eitilt.
Birds of a feather flock together.

Aithneoidh tú iad ar a gcuid oibreacha.
You will recognise them by their works.
(cf. the Bible, Matthew 7:20: 'By their fruits ye shall know them.')

Ritheann an t-ádh go dtí an t-amadán ach ní aithníonn an t-amadán é.
Luck runs to the fool, but the fool does not recognise it.

Geimhreadh ceoch, earrach reoch, samhradh grianmhar is fómhar biamhar.
Winter of mist, a freezing spring, a summer of sun and bountiful autumn
to come.
(i.e. These, according to folklore, are a recognised pattern in the seasons
of Ireland.)

Regret (*Aiféala*)

Ní hé am na hola am na haithrí.
The time of the oil (i.e. the Last Rites) is not the time for repentance.
(cf. Late repentance is not good. i.e. make amends while people are still alive and will appreciate your regret over having wronged them.)

Dá mbeadh breith ar m'aithreachas agam.
If I could undo what I have done.
(lit. 'If I could catch my regret.')

Níl breith ar a nóin ag éinne.
No one can catch the Nones.
('*Nóin*'—Nones, afternoon prayers. cf. What's done is done. i.e. the monk who has missed Nones is unable to catch them; what is past is gone and irretrievable.)

Is leath-chosúil le heireaball an aiféala mar bíonn sí ar an leath deiridh.
Regret is partly like a tail because it's at the end.
('*leath-deiridh*'—backside, rear end)

Pósadh faoi dhithneas; aithreachas go réidh.
Marry in haste; repent at leisure.
(cf. William Congreve, 1670—1729, *The Old Bachelor* (5,8), 'Married in haste, we may repent at leisure.')

Relations (*Gaolta*)

Is tibhe fuil ná uisce.
Blood is thicker than water.

Ní gaol gach Gael.
Every Gael is not a relative.
(i.e. Just because someone shares something in common with you, it does not mean that they are your friend.)

A dó is a dó (sin) mo chol ceathrair.
Two and two is my cousin.
(*Táimid a dó is a dó*—lit. 'We are two and two', which means 'We are cousins'. This is a fun expression which plays on the idiom: *A dó is a dó sin a ceathair*—Two and two are four. It may be used to indicate scorn for some overly complicated explanation of the obvious.)

Bíonn caora dubh i ngach tréad.
There's a black sheep in every flock.

Is sona an bhean a phósann mac na máthar mairbhe.
Happy is the woman who marries the son of a dead mother.

Religion (*Reiligiún*)

Duine gan chreideamh gan náire.
A person without religion/faith is shameless.

Baile, scoil, paróiste.
Home, school, parish.
(An old GAA motto which encouraged young people to grow up through these social institutions, i.e. from the home, through the school, into parish life. Today it is used by an older generation lamenting the loss of traditional values.)

Siúlann an fear óg chun an Aifrinn ach ritheann an seanfhear.
The young man walks to Mass but the old man runs.

Ní bhfaightear uisce coisricthe i dteampall Gallda.
Holy water is not found in a Protestant church.

An té is deise a theach don séipéal is ea an té is moille don Aifreann.
The person who lives closest to the chapel is the latest to arrive at Mass.

Reputation (*Clú*)

An té a chailleann a chlú, cailleann sé a náire.
He who loses his reputation, loses his shame.

Is é an clúmhilleadh an t-olc/an peaca is measa.
Slander is the worst evil/sin.

An té a mbíonn drochchlú air bíonn an bhantracht uile faoina dhéin.
The one who has a bad reputation has all the womenfolk after him.

Caill do chlú agus faigh ar ais é, ach ní hé an rud céanna é.
Lose your reputation and regain it, but it is never the same.

Is minic nach ionann clú agus clí.
It is often that reputation falls short of its manifestation.
(i.e. It is often that reputation does not match reality. cf. '*Clí*'—body,
'*i gclí*'—in the flesh.)

Ní bhíonn uasal ná íseal ach thuas seal agus thíos seal.
There isn't nobility or ignobility, but up a while and down a while.
(i.e. We may be highly respected and successful, but everything is only
for a while. In life, we will also experience failure and being scorned.)

Is fearr dea-chlú ná hallaí óir.
A good reputation is better than halls of gold.

Responsibility (*Freagracht*)

Bíonn gach fear freagrach as a chinniúint féin.
Every man is responsible for his own fate.

Ó chóirigh tú do leaba féin, luigh ar an leaba sin.
Since you made your own bed, lie on that bed.

Is doiligh corrán maith a fháil ar dhrochbhuanaí.
It is hard to find a good sickle for a bad reaper.
(cf. A bad workman always blames his tools.)

Cuir an diallait ar an gcapall ceart.
Put the saddle on the right horse.
(i.e. You're barking up the wrong tree.)

Fear na bó faoina heireaball.
The cow's owner at its tail.
(If a cow falls into a ditch and needs to be pulled out, then the heaviest part of the cow is at its rear end, and so the owner should take the tail as it is he who has most to lose. The proverb urges those who have the biggest stake in any enterprise to take upon themselves the most onerous tasks and not expect others to do it for them.)

Revenge (*Díoltas*)

Súil i gcúiteamh súile, fiacail is gcúiteamh fiacaile.
An eye for an eye; a tooth for a tooth.
(Biblical)

Tiontaigh an leiceann eile.
Turn the other cheek.
(Biblical)

Liomsa an díoltas arsa an Tiarna.
Vengeance is mine, saith the Lord.
(This Biblical quote is sometimes used as a warning to others not to seek revenge as it is only God's prerogative.)

Ná nocht do chuid fiacla go bhféadfaidh tú do ghreim a bhreith.
Don't show your teeth unless you can bite.

Ná maraigh an gadhar de dheasca an tsionnaigh.
Don't kill the dog because of the fox.
(i.e. Because the fox killed one of the sheep, don't take it out on the sheepdog. cf. Don't cut off your nose to spite your face.)

Is milis an rud an díoltas (agus is blasta é bheith fuar).
Revenge is sweet (and it is best served cold).

Is béile fuar gan sásamh an díoltas.
Revenge is a cold meal without satisfaction

242

Sacrifice (*Íobairt*)

Is minic a chaith fear sprot chun breith ar cholmóir.
It is often a man threw a sprat to catch a hake.

Más ábhar peaca duit do shúil, pioc amach í.
If thy eye offend thee, pluck it out.
(Biblical, Matthew 18:9. The actual quote runs: '*Más ábhar peaca duit do shúil, pioc amach agus caith uait í*'—'If thy eye offend thee, pluck it out and cast it from thee.')

Crann le baint anuas chun seolta a chur suas.
A tree has to be knocked down to put up sails.
(i.e. The tree has to be destroyed to make a boat. cf. To make omelets you have to break eggs.)

Níl grá ar bith ann ag fear ar bith is mó ná seo;
an fear a thabharfadh a anam ar son a chairde.
No greater love hath any man than this;
that a man lay down his life for his friends.
(Biblical)

Safety (*Sábháilteacht*)

Aire i gcónaí!
Safety first!

Cluiche faichilleach an imirt.
The way to win the game is to play it safe.

Ní neart go teacht le chéile.
There isn't strength till getting together.
(cf. There is safety in numbers.)

Is fearr go cúramach ná go deo.
Better carefully than never.
(cf. Better safe than sorry.)

Is mall gach cos ar chosán gan eolas.
Every foot is slow on an unknown footpath.
(i.e. Care must be taken in any task that is being undertaken for the first time.)

Is maith an sciath líon an tí in aghaidh drochní.
The household (together) is a good shield against evil things.
(cf. There is safety in numbers.)

Sea (*Farraige*)

Bíonn súil leis an fharraige.
The sea offers hope.
(Often continued: *ach ní bhíonn súil leis an uaigh—*
but the grave offers no hope.)

Faigheann an fharraige a cuid féin.
The sea receives its own.

Ná déan dánaíocht ar an bhfarraige.
Don't make bold with the sea.
(i.e. The sea is a dangerous and powerful adversary.)

Is bádóir oilte gach fear is an fharraige ina chlár.
Every man is a skilled boatman in a calm sea.

Is iomaí bád a cailleadh i bhfarraige ciúin.
It's many the boat has been lost in a quiet sea.
(i.e. The sea may look harmless but it has many hidden dangers.)

Is deacair droim ina haonar leis an bhfarraige mhór.
One single back against the open sea is difficult.
(i.e. One person or a handful of people cannot stop the inevitable.)

Má chuireann báid gráin ort, ná tóg teach cois farraige.
If you hate boats, don't build a house by the sea.
(i.e. Don't put yourself in a situation that will cause you distress.)

Tá lán mara eile san fharraige.
There is another tide in the sea.

Bádh an long de dheasca aon pheacaí amháin.
The ship was sunk because of one sinner.
(i.e. It only takes the actions of one foolish person
to decide the fate of many.)

Tá iasc san fharraige chomh maith is a gabhadh ann fós.
There is a fish in the sea as good as any that has been caught.
(cf. There are plenty more fish in the sea.)

Is ainmhí clóis talamh is tír ach is beithíoch buile an mhuir.
The land can be domesticated, but the sea is a raging beast.
(i.e. No one is master of the sea.)

Tá bia fós san fharraige nuair a bhíonn gorta agus gátar sa ghort.
There is food still in the sea when there is want and famine in the field.
(i.e. The sea is a last resort for the supply of food when all other sources have
failed. Much useful flotsam and jetsam arrived on shore from shipwrecks.
Tomás Ó Criomhthain alludes to the importance of this in *The Islander:*
'There wouldn't be anyone alive on the island today if it hadn't been for the
shipwrecks, and of course the old hag used to say that it was God who had
sent them to the poor.')

Seasons (*Ráithe*)

Ráithe an earraigh, ráite an ghrá.
The season of spring is for utterances of love.

Is fearr dhá lá san earrach ná deich lá san fhómhar.
Two days in spring is better than ten days in the autumn.

Grá, ceol agus ríl in earrach an tsaoil.
Love, music and dancing in the spring of life.
(cf. Gather ye rosebuds while ye may.)

Sábháil an fómhar fad is a bhíonn an ghrian thuas.
Save the harvest while the sun is up.
(cf. Make hay while the sun shines.)

I lár an tsamhraidh saor ó bheann ní chreidimid go dtiocfaidh fuacht an tseaca anuas ar ár gceann.
In the midst of summer free from care, we do not believe the frosty cold will fall upon our heads.
(i.e. Don't be deluded by the allure of bright summer days as tougher times will surely arrive.)

Ní hiad na fir mhóra a bhaineann an fómhar.
It isn't the big men who reap the harvest.
(cf. The best goods come in small parcels.)

Geimhreadh ceoch, earrach reoch, samhradh grianmhar is fómhar biamhar.
Winter of mist, a freezing spring, a summer of sun and bountiful autumn to come.
(i.e. These, according to folklore, are a recognised pattern in the seasons of Ireland.)

Lá millte na móna lá fómhar an chabáiste.
The rain that destroys the turf can cause cabbages to grow.
(i.e. What is bad for one thing is good for another. cf. One man's meat is another man's poison.)

Bíonn a shéasúr féin ag gach rud.
To everything there is a season.
(Biblical)

Bíonn a shonas féin ag gach séasúr (ach amháin geimhreadh gan deireadh.)
Every season has its own joy (except a winter that is too long).
(i.e. Youth is a joyful season of expectation, as old age is a time when a person can look back and the enjoy fruits of life's labors. However, if old age continues too long then it can eventually lose its joy.)

Is ionann séasúr na ronnach agus biaiste na maicréal.
The season of the mackerel is the same as the season of the mackerel.
(cf. It is six of one and half a dozen of the other. i.e. It is all the same.)

Secret (*Rún*)

Rachaidh rún chun na huaighe.
A secret will go to the grave.

Ní scéal rúin a chuala triúr.
It isn't a secret if three know.

Coinníonn triúr rún má tá beirt acu marbh.
Three keep a secret if two of the three are dead.

Bíonn cluasa ar na claíocha.
There are ears on the ditches.
(i.e. It isn't safe to speak about your secrets aloud.)

Ná lig do rún le claí.
Do not tell your secret to a fence.
(i.e. Tell nobody your secret.)

Más eol do thriúr ní rún é.
If three know it, it is not a secret.

Self (*Féin*)

Mé féineachas.
Selfishness.
(lit. 'Myself-ness'—said about someone who is involved in a totally self-ish endeavour to the detriment of others.)

Gach duine ar a shon féin!
Everyone for themselves!

Bí fírinneach duit féin.
Be true to yourself.

Cuidíonn Dia leo siúd a gcuidíonn leo féin.
('God helps those who help themselves.'—attributed to Benjamin Franklin (1706—1790), but translated from an earlier French source.)

Is dall an grá baoth.
Self-love is blind.

Tusa domsa, mise duit, sinn dúinne go léir!
You for me and I for you, we for all of us together!
(cf. All for one and one for all!)

Creideann gach baile gurb é croílár na hÉireann é.
Every town thinks it is the hub of Ireland.
('*croí*'—heart/centre of activity. i.e. Everyone thinks they are the centre of the universe.)

Sense (*Ciall*)

Ní thagann gaois roimh aois.
You can't put an old head on young shoulders.

Ní dheachaigh rogha riamh ó réiteach.
There is no better choice than reconciliation.
(i.e. Making peace wherever possible is always sensible.)

Ní thagann ciall roimh aois.
Sense doesn't come before age.

Níl ciall ag an ghrá.
Love has no sense.

Ní ciallmhar i gcónaí an rud a mbíonn ciall leis.
What's sensible isn't always the sensible thing.

Is í an chiall cheannaithe an chiall is fearr.
Sense that is bought (by experience) is the best sense.
(i.e. People can't be told.)

Ní taisce ciall an chiall in aisce.
Sense has no value unless attained though personal experience.
(i.e. Experience is the only true teacher.)

Is deacair giorria a chur as tor nuair nach bhfuil sé ann.
It's hard to get a hare out of a bush when he's not there.
(i.e. If there is no sense in a person, there is no sense in looking for sense in the senseless person.)

Shame (*Náire*)

Ní náire an bhochtaineacht.
Poverty is not shame.

Is náire an saibhreas agus an daibhreas ag an gheata.
Wealth is shame while poverty is at the gate.

Dorn de shó agus lán baile de náire.
A fist full of dosh/cash is worth a full village of shame.

An té a chaill a oineach ní bhíonn náire air.
The one who has lost his honour is shameless.

Is ball buan den donas an náire.
Shame is a constant component of poverty.

Silence (*Tost*)

Is binn béal ina thost.
A silent mouth is sweet.

Focal airgead—ciúine ór!
Speech is silver—silence is gold.

Is minic ciúin ciontach.
The silent one is usually the guilty one.

Déanann ceann ciallmhar béal iata.
A wise man keeps his counsel.

Seachain an duine a bhíonn ina thost.
Avoid the person of few words.

Ní dhearna ciúin botún.
Silence didn't make a mistake.

Ritheann uiscí doimhne ciúin.
Deep waters run quietly.
(cf. Still waters run deep.)

Similarity (*Cosúlacht*)

Cad a dhéanfaidh mac an chait ach luch a mharú?
What will the son of the cat do but kill a mouse?
(cf. Like father, like son.)

Tuigeann fáidh fáidh eile.
One prophet understands another prophet.
(cf. Great minds think alike.)

Aithníonn ciaróg ciaróg eile.
One beetle recognises another beetle.
(cf. Birds of a feather flock together.)

Más ionúin an chráin is ionúin an t-ál.
If the sow is beloved then the litter is beloved.
(i.e. If one is to be loved, so is the other. cf. Love me, love my dog.)

Más fuar an teachtaireacht, is fuar an freagra.
If the messenger is cold, the answer is cold.

Sin (*Peaca*)

An té atá saor ó pheaca caitheadh seisean an chéad chloch.
He who is without sin, let him throw the first stone.
(Biblical, John 8:7. The actual wording is: '*An duine atá saor ó pheaca eadraibh caitheadh seisean an chéad chloch léi*—'The person who is free from sin amongst you, let him throw the first stone at her.')

Bádh an long de dheasca aon pheacaí amháin.
The ship was sunk because of one sinner.
(i.e. It only takes the actions of one foolish person to decide the fate of many.)

Ní peaca an tseanaois; ní suáilce an óige.
Old age isn't a sin; youth isn't a virtue.

Ní peaca guí a iarraidh.
It's not a sin to ask.

Is peacach giolla na leisce baoithe ach is measa fós bheith ar meisce choíche.
A sinner the lad who is foolishly lazy, but worse by far is the sinner who is endlessly drunk.

Skill (*Scil/Ceird*)

Is namhaid ceird mura gcleachtar í.
A skill becomes an enemy if it isn't practised.

Ceileann cleachtadh crua castacht ceirde.
Hard practice hides the difficulty of a skill.
(i.e. Slogging away at practice makes what is difficult look easy.)

Bíonn gach rud éasca nuair a bhíonn an cleas ar eolas agat.
Everything is easy when you know the trick.

Tagann gach ceird le cleachtadh.
Every trade/skill comes with practice.

Sna farraigí suaite atá foghlaim na bádóireachta.
The skill of boating is learnt in choppy seas.

Foireann dhochloíte is ea cumas le cleachtadh.
Talent and practice become an unbeatable team.

Sleep (*Codladh*)

Cara caoin an codladh.
Sleep is a gentle friend.

Dochtúir na sláinte an codladh.
Sleep is the doctor of health.

Deartháir don bhás an codladh.
Sleep is a brother to death.

Tosach na sláinte an codladh.
The beginning of recovery is sleep.

Scéal do chapall ina chodladh é.
A story being told to a horse that's asleep.
(i.e. The listener has no interest in the story being told.)

Bás beag (is ea) an codladh.
Sleep is a little death.

Snow (*Sneachta*)

Nuair atá sneachta ar Néifinn tá sé fuar in Éirinn.
When there is snow on Nephin it's cold in Ireland.
(Nephin Mountain is situated in County Mayo, and is believed to be a
good indicator of the weather in Ireland.)

Leasú seacht mbliana brúcht mhaith sneachta.
A good fall of snow fertilises the soil for seven years.

Geimhreadh gan sneachta ná sioc ina luí,
fómhar galrach agus tinneas sa tigh.
A winter without snow or frost on the ground (means) an unhealthy
harvest and sickness in the house.

Bíonn taithí ag na sléibhte ar an sneachta.
The mountains are used to snow.

Deir gach calóg sa mhaidhm shneachta nárbh uirthi (go raibh) aon locht.
Every snowflake in the avalanche pleads its innocence.

Sorrow (*Brón*)

Níl cara ag cumha ach cuimhne.
Sadness has no friend but memory.

An té atá brónach ní geal fiú an ghrian.
To him who is sorrowful, not even the sun is bright.

Tagann an ghrian i ndiaidh na fearthainne.
The sun arrives after the rain.
(i.e. All sorrows will pass, and will be followed by joy.)

Scéal gealgháireach ó chroí briste brónach.
A cheerful story from a sad heart.
(i.e. Often a person might be sorrowful, but they cover their sadness by speaking in a cheerful manner.)

Ní fada ár n-óige shona faoin ngréin go dtagann an tseanaois, an chaill agus léan.
Not for long is our youth happy and sunny before old age, loss and sadness arrive.

Tuigeann gach duine cá luíonn an bhróg air.
Everyone knows where the shoe pinches him.
(i.e. We all have our own private sorrows of which others are not aware.)

Speech (*Caint*)

Beagán a rá agus a rá go maith.
Say a little and say it well.

Is minic a bhris béal duine a shrón.
It is often that someone's mouth broke their nose.

Níor bhris dea-fhocal béal éinne riamh.
A kind word never broke anyone's mouth.

An té is ciúine is buaine.
The one who is quieter will last longer.

Is mó duine a labhair go minic ach nach ndúirt tada.
Many a person has spoken but said nothing.
(*Tagann Godot*, Alan Titley, 1947—)

Is mó duine nár labhair focal ach a dúirt a lán.
Many a person never spoke a word but said a lot.
(*Tagann Godot*, Alan Titley, 1947—)

Strength (*Neart*)

Ní neart go teacht le chéile.
There is no strength till getting it together.
(cf. There is strength in unity/Together we stand, divided we fall.)

Tá an ceart ag an neart.
Might is right.

An té nach bhfuil ceann láidir air ní mór dó cosa láidre a bheith faoi.
He who hasn't a good head must have strong legs.
(i.e. If you have a poor memory, or are scatterbrained, you will have to do a lot more walking.)

Bíonn cosa crua faoi chapall na comharsan.
The neighbour's horse has strong legs.
(i.e. Used when referring to the mistreatment of something borrowed, or disrespect for another's property. One takes better care of one's own horse than one's neighbour's.)

Is treise dúchas ná oiliúint.
Nature is stronger than nurture.

Substitution (*Ionadaíocht*)

Cor in aghaidh an chaim.
A twist in place of the bend.
('*cam*'—crooked act. cf. Tit for tat.)

Sop in áit na scuaibe.
A straw in place of the brush.
(i.e. an inadequate replacement)

Clúdaigh an scáthán ar eagla an mhalartáin,
Is tlú ar an gcliabhán mar chaomhnú an leanbáin.
Cover the mirror for fear of the changeling,
And the tongs on the cot to protect the infant.
(These were traditional superstitions in rural Ireland, where placing tongs
on a cot or putting a cover on the mirror prevented the *lucht sí* ('the fairy
people') from coming into your house and placing a *malartán* ('changeling') in the place of the real baby. The changeling would cry constantly
and cause trouble and misery to the whole household.)

Is minic gur fearr bheith in aice le duine ná ina ionad.
Often it is better to be assisting rather than being in charge.

Success (*Rath*)

Caitheann síor-shileadh an chloch.
Continuous weathering wears the rock down.
(i.e. Perseverance brings success.)

Ní bhíonn an rath ach mar a mbíonn an smacht.
There is no success without discipline.

An té a mbíonn an t-ádh ar maidin air bíonn sé air maidin is tráthnóna.
The one who is lucky in the morning is lucky in the morning and the afternoon.
(cf. Success breeds success/Nothing succeeds like success.)

Ní féidir gach cluiche a thabhairt leat.
You can't win every game.
(cf. You can't win 'em all!)

Múinteoir mall an rath ach is maith an t-oide teip.
Success is a sluggish teacher, but failure is a good tutor.
(Usually only the second half is said: '*Is maith an t-oide teip.*')

Suffering (*Fulaingt*)

Níl pá gan chrá.
There is no pay without torment.
(cf. No pain, no gain.)

Ní bhíonn bua gan dua.
There isn't any victory without effort.

Bíonn crosa roimh chách.
There are crosses before everyone.
(i.e. Everyone has their own difficulties.)

Bíonn cros le hiompar ag gach duine.
Everyone has their cross to bear.

Tá a fhios ag gach éinne cá ngoilleann an bhróg air.
Everyone knows where the shoe pinches him.
(i.e. Everyone has their own difficulties of which we are not aware.)

Saol fada fulaingt fhada.
A long life means lengthy suffering.

Superstition (*Piseog*)

Ná téigh chun farraige má chastar sagart ort sa treo.
Don't go to sea if you meet a priest on the way.
(Meeting a priest, a nun or a red-haired woman on the way to the sea was considered an ill-omen.)

Cat dubh (romhat) ar an ród agus amhantar áidh ag imeacht le scód!
A black cat before you on the road and a lucky venture will take wing.

An té a mbíonn an t-ádh ar maidin air bíonn sé air maidin is tráthnóna.
The one who is lucky in the morning is lucky in the morning and the afternoon.

Is olc an comhartha éadach glas.
It's an evil sign, green clothing.
(Irish people were often worried about wearing any green-coloured clothing, and when they did they frequently also wore some kind of charm in order to ward off any harmful influences. Men, for example, would wear two small crossed twigs behind the lapel of their jacket.)

Spéir dhearg istoíche rath agus séan,
Spéir dhearg ar maidin feánna léin.
A red sky at night means success and prosperity,
A red sky in the morning means fathoms of woe.

Tá eireaball an chait sa ghríosach.
The cat's tail is in the embers.
(i.e. Bad weather is on the way.)

Go raibh Brat Bhríde dár gcaomhnú ar dhrochíde!
May the Cloth of Brigid preserve us from maltreatment!
(On 31 January, the eve of the Feast of St Brigid, a piece of cloth is left outside the house on a fence or hedge, where according to tradition the saint blesses it as she passes by during the night. This cloth, known as 'Brat Bhríde', is then believed to have been imbued with magical powers.)

Clúdaigh an scáthán ar eagla an mhalartáin,
Is tlú ar an gcliabhán mar chaomhnú an leanbáin.
Cover the mirror for fear of the changeling,
And the tongs on the cot to protect the infant.
(These were traditional superstitions in rural Ireland where placing tongs on a cot or putting a cover on the mirror prevented the *lucht sí* ('the fairy people') from coming into your house and placing a *malartán* ('changeling') in place of the real baby. The changeling would cry constantly and cause trouble and misery to the whole household.)

Fanadh an dreoilín go fóillín!
Let the little wren wait for a little while!
(cf. Hold your horses! Used when asking someone to be quiet until a danger has passed, or until they properly understand the situation. This refers to a belief that a wren's chirping and tapping on the drums of the Irish soldiers gave their position away to Cromwell's army. Alerted by the bird, Cromwell's men massacred all the Irish. To this day in Kerry, '*Lá an Dreoilín*' ('Wren Day') is celebrated on 26 December, when children go from house to house asking for money to bury their wren.)

Poll dóite tuar pósta.
A burnt hole (in a person's clothes) is a sign of getting married soon.

Talk (*Caint*)

Amhail píb mhála an fear; ní sheinneann sé go mbeidh a bholg lán.
A man is like a bagpipe—he doesn't make a noise until his belly's full.
('*ní sheinneann sé*'—'he doesn't sing', but here it means 'there isn't a squeak out of him.')

Ní líontar an bolg le caint.
Talk doesn't fill the belly.

Is fusa a rá ná a dhéanamh.
It is easier said than done.

Téann focail le gaoth.
Words are just wind.
(cf. Talk is cheap.)

Is fearr an t-aon ghníomh amháin ná céad focal.
One action is better than a thousand words.
(cf. Walk the talk.)

Focal mór agus droch-chur leis.
Big words and little action.
(cf. Big on talk; small on action.)

Tea (*Tae*)

Marbh le tae agus marbh gan é.
Dead with the tea and dead without it.

Is cuma le tae cé a ólfas é.
Tea doesn't mind who drinks it.

Taephota sa teallach, 'sé a shásóidh an chailleach.
A teapot on the stove is what will please an old woman.

An cupán tae—sólás an lae.
A cup of tea—(provides a moment of) solace during the day.

Is é an t-am is fearr chun tae a ól ná am ar bith.
The best time to drink tea is any time at all.

Ól an tae agus ná téigh 'un óil.
Drink tea and don't go off drinking (alcohol).
(A slogan to encourage people to refrain from consuming alcohol.)

Thrift (*Tíos*)

Bailíonn brobh beart.
Every little counts.
(cf. 'Many a little makes a mickle.')

Is mór (iad) na beaganna i dteannta a chéile.
All the little things add up.

Is é cosaint na pingine a chruachas na puint.
Look after the pennies and the pounds will look after themselves.

Tíos na pingine agus cur amú na scillinge.
Penny-wise and pound-foolish.

Ná bí caifeach agus ní bheidh tú gann.
Waste not, want not.

Ó loisc tú an choinneal, loisc an t-orlach.
Since you burnt the candle, burn the inch.
(cf. In for a penny, in for a pound.)

Déan do chonradh de réir do spáráin.
Make your contract according to your purse.
(i.e. Live within your means.)

Time (*Am*)

Is maith an scéalaí an aimsir.
Time will tell.

Is maith an lia an t-am.
Time heals.

Ní féidir an dá thrá a fhreastal.
You can't be in two places at the same time.

Tamall gan treoir—tamall na ndeor.
Time without direction is a time of tears.

Is fearr mall ná go brách.
Better late than never.

Seal na póige mí na Riabhóige.
April is kissing time.

Fainic an fuílleach i mí na bhfaoilleach!
Take care of the residue in the month of February.
(i.e. As February is a harsh winter month, do not be too extravagant with
the remainder of the fuel and food reserves.)

An rud is annamh is iontaí.
The thing that is rare is most wonderful.

Ní fhanann trá le héinne.
The tide waits for no one.
(cf. Time and tide wait for no man.)

Ní fhanann uain ná taoide le haon duine.
Opportunity and tide wait for no person.

Mol an lá um thráthnóna.
Praise the day in the afternoon.

Beidh lá eile ag an bPaorach.
Mr Power will have another day.
(i.e. Maybe this time success was not within reach, but eventually success
will arrive one day. cf. Tomorrow is another day!)

Céad gnó céad ló.
A hundred jobs—a hundred days.
(i.e. There is no point in rushing things.)

Éasca nóin ná maidin.
Afternoon is easier than morning.

Travel (*Taisteal*)

Giorraíonn beirt bóthar.
Two shorten the road.

Is fada an bóthar gan casadh.
It is a long road that has no turn.

Ní bhíonn conair gan ceann.
Every journey (lit. path) has its end.

Is glas iad na cnoic i bhfad uainn.
Faraway hills are green.

Bíonn siúlach scéalach.
The traveler has many stories.
(cf. Travel broadens the mind.)

Is iomaí fear a thóg idir chorp agus anam leis go tíortha i gcéin ach a d'fhág a chroí sa bhaile.
It is many the man who has gone both body and soul to foreign lands, but left his heart at home.

Trees (*Crainn*)

Dá mbeifeá chomh láidir le crann darach, gheobhaidh an bás an ceann is fearr ort.
Even if you are as strong as an oak, death will get the better of you.

Mar a leagtar an crann is ann a bhíonn na slisneacha.
Where the tree is felled, that's where the chippings are.
(i.e. Don't overlook what is obvious.)

Is san adhmad is boige a bhíonn an tsnaidhm is crua.
It is in the softest wood that the hardest knot is found.
(i.e. Someone may look like an old softy, but underneath there may be an iron core.)

Maireann an crann ach ní mhaireann an lámh a chuir é.
The tree lives, but the hand that planted it does not.
(i.e. Actions that bring life live on after the demise of their instigators.)

Faoi bhun an chrainn a thiteann na duilleoga.
It is at the foot of the tree the leaves fall.

Cá mbeadh úll ach mar a mbeadh an abhaill.
Where would an apple be but where the apple-tree is?

Níl coill ar bith ann gan a loisceadh féin de chríonach inti.
There is no forest without enough dead wood in it to burn itself down.
('*críonach*'—decayed wood)

Triads (*Tréanna*)

Triúr fear nach dtuigeann na mná: fir óga, fir aosta agus fir mheán-aosta.
Three sorts of men who do not understand women: young men, old men
and middle-aged men.

Trí ní nach féidir a cheilt: tart, tochas agus ocras.
Three things you cannot hide: thirst, an itch and hunger.

*Tá trí shaghas ban ann: bean chomh mí-náireach le muc, bean chomh crosta
le cearc, agus bean chomh mín leis an uan.*
There are three kinds of women: a woman as shameless as a pig, a woman
as contrary as a hen and a woman as gentle as a lamb.

Trí ní nach mothaítear ag teacht: cíos, aois agus féasóg.
Three things you don't notice arriving: rent, age and a beard.

Trí ní gur ceart a sheachaint: ceann saighde, béal gunna, agus teanga mná.
Three things you should avoid: the head of an arrow, the mouth of a gun
and a woman's tongue.

Trí airí na ceanntréine: cuairteanna síoraí, stánadh síoraí, agus ceisteanna síoraí.
Three characteristics of obstinacy: endless visiting, endless staring and
endless questions.

Trí airí de ghrá an óig; stánadh síoraí, easpa codlata, agus tost.
Three characteristics of a youth in love: constant staring, loss of sleep and
being silent.

Trí ní a chuireann imní ar bhean an tí: cnag déanach an tsagairt ar dhoras an tí, cnag mhná sí i lár na hoích', glothar báis a fir in ísle brí.
Three things that worry the woman of the house: the late knock of the priest on her door, the knock of the banshee in the middle of the night, and the death-rattle of her enfeebled husband.

Trí airí an dea-áidh: gáire an linbh óig, gol an chitil agus glór na mná mánla.
Three characteristics of good fortune: the laughter of a young child, the crying of a kettle and the voice of a gentle woman.

Trí nach féidir a sheachaint: aicíd, aois agus bás
Three things that cannot be avoided: illness, age and death.

Triúr fear nach cóir pósadh: lúbaire, diúgaire agus fear mire.
Three men that shouldn't get married: a deceitful person, a drunkard or a madman.

Trí ní gur cóir a lorg i mbean chéile: macántacht, maighdeanas agus máchail.
Three things you should look for in a wife: honesty, purity and a defect/fault.

Triúr bean a thugann an mí-ádh leo: bean gan náire, bean gan gáire, bean gan cúram tí.
Three sorts of women who bring ill-luck: a shameless woman, a woman who does not laugh and an idle woman.

Trí ní ba chóir bheith agat: beannacht do mháthar, foighne mhic Dé agus ádh an diabhail.
Three things that you should have: the blessing of your mother, the patience of the Son of God and the luck of the Devil.

Trick (*Cleas*)

Is maith an cleas an cleamhnas.
Marriage is a good trick.

Níl cleas gan cluain.
Every trick has deception in it.

Ní cleas é go ndéantar trí huaire é.
It isn't a trick until it has been done three times.

Cleas nó cóisir!
Trick or treat!
(Catchphrase used at Hallowe'en by children in fancy dress, who call from door to door collecting sweets, fruits and nuts.)

Is deacair cleas nua a mhúineadh do sheanghadhar.
It is hard to teach an old dog new tricks.

Bíonn cleasa le foghlaim i ngach ceird.
There are tricks in all trades.

Trust and Treachery
(*Iontaoibh agus Feall*)

Ná tabhair taobh le fear fala.
Do not trust a spiteful man.

Sionnach i gcraiceann an uain.
A fox in a lamb's skin.

Trí rud nach iontaoibh: lá breá sa gheimhreadh, trócaire na mara, nó dea-ghlór mná.
Three things not to be trusted: a fine day in the winter, mercy from the sea, and the kindly voice of a woman.

Filleann an feall ar an bhfeallaire.
The evil deed returns on the evildoer.

Deacair taobh a thabhairt leis na mná.
It is difficult to trust a woman.

Bíonn creideamh ag laoch ach ní creideamh caoch.
Have trust, but make sure.
(cf. Russian Proverb: Доверяй, но проверяй.)

Truth and Lies
(*Fírinne agus Bréaga*)

Bíonn dhá chos ar bhréag ach ní bhíonn ach leathchos ar an fhírinne.
A lie has two feet but the truth walks lame

Is cuairteoir déanach an fhírinne ach tiocfaidh gan gó.
The truth is a late visitor but a sure one.

Imíonn bréag ach fanann an fhírinne.
A lie passes away but the truth remains.

Ní mhaireann bréag ach tamall.
A lie only endures a while.

Bia an bhoicht bréag.
A lie is food for the poor.

Is minic gur searbh an fhírinne ach is milis an bhréag bheag ar uaire.
Truth is often bitter, and a small lie can sometimes be sweet.

Mór í an fhírinne agus buafaidh sí.
Truth is great and will prevail.
(i.e. The truth will always out.)

Ní féidir an dubh a chur ina gheal ach seal.
You can't deny the truth but for a while.
(i.e. You can't keep calling black white.)

Is deacair don fhírinne leaba a fháil.
It is hard for the truth to find a bed.
(i.e. It is hard for the truth to find a home.)

Beathú an staraí an fhírinne.
The nourishment of the historian is truth.

Gheobhair gan gó ar chlog neamhbheo an t-am ceart dhá uair sa ló.
Truly you will get the right time from a stopped clock twice a day.
(cf. Even a stopped clock is right twice a day.)

Is féidir bréag a rá leis an fhírinne a insint.
A lie can be told by telling the truth.
(i.e. The truth can be presented in such a way as
to create a false understanding of the facts.)

Bíonn cuid den fhírinne i ngach bréag.
Every lie has some truth in it.
(cf. Geoffrey Chaucer, 1343—1400, *The Canterbury Tales*, The Cook's
Tale: 'A man may full sooth in game and play.' Similarly William
Shakespeare, 1582—1616, *King Lear* (5,3), 'Jesters do oft prove proph-
ets.' Cf. Many a true word is spoken in jest.)

Tá fírinní ann nach mbaineann le fírící.
There exist truths that have nothing to do with facts.

Value/Worth (*Luach/Fiúntas*)

Is binn blas ar an mbeagán.
Small amounts are sweet.

Is fearr breac sa láimh ná bradán sa linn.
A trout in the hand is worth a salmon in the pool.

Ní tréad caora.
One sheep is not a flock.

An rud is annamh is iontach.
The rare thing is a thing of wonder.

Ní sheasann sac folamh.
An empty sack doesn't stand.

An rud nach fiú a lorg, ní fiú a fháil.
The thing that is not worth seeking is not worth getting.

Ní raibh cuibheasach in a thaoiseach maith riamh.
Mediocre never makes a good leader.

Ceannaigh drochrud agus beidh tú gan aon rud.
Buy a bad thing and you will be without anything.

Is fearr an mhaith bheag atá ná an mhaith mhór a bhí.
The small good thing that is here now is better that the big good thing
that was.
(i.e. Live in the 'now' and enjoy the good things that are present today.)

Is fearr madra beo ná leon marbh.
A live dog is better than a dead lion.

Is fearr greim amháin de choinín ná dhá ghreim de chat.
One bite of a rabbit is better than two bites of a cat.

Ná loit an díon de dheasca easpa dornáin den tuí.
Don't spoil the roof for want of a handful of straw.
(cf. Don't spoil the ship/sheep for a ha'porth of tar.)

Níl maith sa seanchas nuair a bhíos an anachain déanta.
There is not good in talking when the harm has been done.
(cf. No good crying over spilt milk.)

Rud inniu nach saol gan é—amárach ní fiú mallacht Dé.
Something today that is greatly valued, tomorrow isn't worth a curse.

Is olc an cú nach fiú a liú.
It's a poor hound that isn't worth calling.

Fios ar phraghas de gach rud ach a luach gan bheith ar eolas agat.
To know the price of everything but the value of nothing.
(cf. A cynic is 'a man who knows the price of everything and the value of nothing.' Oscar Wilde, 1854—1900, *Lady Windermere's Fan*. Wilde also provides the reply of course: 'And a sentimentalist ... is a man who sees an absurd value in everything, and doesn't know the market price of any single thing.')

Victory (*Bua*)

Ní bhíonn bua mór gan chontúirt.
There is never great victory without great danger.

Níl bua gan dua.
There is no victory without hardship.
(cf. No pain, no gain!)

Bíonn gach bua ina sheasamh ar choirp an díomua.
Every victory stands on the corpses of failure.
(i.e. In order to succeed, we must fail many times.)

A bháis, cá bhfuil do bhua?
A éag, cá bhfuil do chealg?
O grave, where is thy sting?
O death, where is thy victory?
(Biblical, from 1 Corinthians, 15:55, King James Version)

Dhá dtrian den bhua—dealramh.
Two thirds of victory is appearance.

Maitheas agus bua ó mhaitheamh croí is trua.
Property and victory from forgiveness and compassion.

Water (*Uisce*)

Ritheann uiscí doimhne ciúin.
Deep waters run quietly.
(cf. Still waters run deep.)

Is é an sruthán éadomhain a labhraíonn go dána.
It is the shallow stream that speaks boldly.
(cf. Empty vessels make the most noise.)

Fuaim ard na n-uiscí éadroma.
Loud noise from shallow waters.

Gach duine ag tarraingt uisce ar a mhuileann féin.
Everyone bringing water to their own mill.
(i.e. Everyone looking after their own interests. cf. I'm all right, Jack.)

Dá mhéad an tuile, tránn sí.
However great the flood, it will ebb.

Wealth (*Saibhreas/Maoin*)

Ní thuigeann saibhir daibhir.
A rich man never understands a poor man.

Is fearr clú ná conách.
Character/reputation is better than wealth.

Sparán trom—croí éadrom.
A heavy purse makes for a light heart.

Is minic a bhíonn saibhir bocht.
It is often the wealthy are poor.

Déanann ciste cairdeas.
Wealth makes friendship.

Bíonn an saibhreas sa chroí, ní sa sparán.
Wealth is in the heart, not in the purse.

Is fusa do chamall dul trí chró snáthaide ná
do dhuine saibhir dul isteach i ríocht Dé.
It is easier for a camel to go through the eye of a needle than for a rich
man to enter the kingdom of God.
(Biblical)

Weather (*Aimsir*)

Teas gaoithe aduaidh nó fuacht gaoithe aneas, sin báisteach.
The north wind's heat or the cold of the south wind means rain

Dearg aniar—soineann is grian,
Dearg anoir—sneachta is sioc,
Dearg aneas—doineann is teas,
Dearg aduaidh—clagairt is fuacht.
Red in the west—fine weather and sun,
Red in the east—snow 'n frost to come,
Red in the south—means storm and heat,
Red in the north—brings the cold and sleet.

Níor tháinig stoirm riamh gan báisteach ina dhiaidh.
A storm never comes that doesn't bring rain after it.

Is maith an cúnamh lá breá.
It is a good help an fine day.
(cf. A bright day brightens the spirit.)

Geimhreadh ceoch, earrach reoch, samhradh grianmhar is fómhar biamhar.
Winter of mist, a freezing spring, a summer of sun and bountiful autumn
to come.
(i.e. According to folklore, these are a recognised pattern in the seasons
of Ireland.)

Caitheann síor-shileadh an chloch.
Continuous weathering wears the rock down.
(i.e. Perseverance brings success.)

Tá eireaball an chait sa ghríosach.
The cat's tail is in the embers.
(i.e. Bad weather is on the way.)

Lá millte na móna lá fómhar an chabáiste.
The rain that destroys the turf can cause cabbage to grow.
(i.e. What is bad for one thing is good for another. cf. One man's meat is
another man's poison.)

*Is mairg don té a fhaigheann bás san fhearthainn mar tagann an ghrian
amach ina dhiaidh.*
Woe to him who dies in the rain, for the sun comes out afterwards.
(i.e. If times are difficult, fight on; there are brighter times to come.)

Tar éis doininne tig soineann.
After bad weather comes fine skies.

Cothú na doininne soineann na hoíche.
A calm night presages a storm.
(cf. The calm before the storm.)

Will (*Toil*)

An té ag a mbíonn an toil bíonn an tslí.
Where there's a will, there's a way.

Is treise toil ná tuiscint.
Will is stronger than understanding.

Is fearr tuiscint agus léann seachas sotal agus toil tréan.
Learning and understanding is better than arrogance and a strong will.

Is minic gur fearr an toil ná an t-eolas.
Willpower is often better than know-how.

Gabhann toil chun troda, gabhann an géilleadh gean.
Will turns to fighting; compromise wins affection.

Beatha duine a thoil.
A person's (free) will is their life.
(i.e. Everyone should be allowed to choose for themselves.)

Wisdom (*Gaois*)

Ní bhíonn gaois roimh aois.
Wisdom doesn't come before age.

Ní bhíonn an duine críonna go dtéann an beart thart.
A person is not wise until the deed is done.

Ní haon ualach an chiall.
Good sense is no burden.

Níl saoi gan locht.
There isn't a wise man who hasn't got some fault.

Is dóigh le fear gan chiall gurb é fear na céille é.
The one without sense imagines that he is the one with sense.

Tar éis a thuigtear gach beart.
It is easy to be wise after the event.

Wives and Women (*Mná*)

Ní fear go bean chéile.
A man's not a man till he gets a wife.

Na trí éirí is measa le déanamh: éirí ó Aifreann gan chríochnú, éirí ó bhord gan altú, éirí ó leaba do mhná féin chun a hathrú.
The three worst risings to be made: rising from Mass before its end, rising from the table not having said grace, and rising from the bed of your own wife to go to another.

Glacann drochbhean comhairle gach fir ach a fir féin.
A bad wife takes the advice of every man except her husband.

Ná gabh bean gan máchail/gan locht.
Don't take as a wife a woman without a blemish/without a fault.

Fianaise an ghiolla bhréagaigh a bhean.
The lying man's witness is his wife.

Níl ní níos géire ná teanga mná.
There is nothing sharper than a woman's tongue.

Triúr fear go dteipeann orthu mná a thuiscint: fir óga, fir aosta agus fir mheánaosta.
Three kinds of men who fail to understand women: young men, old men and middle-aged men.

Words (*Focail/Briathra*)

Níor bhris focal maith fiacail riamh.
A good word never broke a tooth.
(cf. A kind word never hurt anybody.)

Tuigeann fear léinn leathfhocal.
A learned man understands half a word.
(i.e. A word to the wise is sufficient.)

Téann focail le gaoth.
Words are just wind.
(cf. Talk is cheap.)

Focal mór agus droch-chur leis.
Big words and little action.
(cf. Big on talk; small on action.)

Is fearr focal sa chúirt ná bonn sa sparán.
Better to have a word in court than a coin in your purse.
(i.e. Influence is more valuable than money.)

Ní chothaíonn na briathra na bráithre.
Words do not nourish the brothers.
(cf. Fair words butter no parsnips.)

Ní briathar a dhearbhaíos ach gníomh.
It is not a word that proves, but an action.
(cf. Actions speak louder than words.)

Work/Employment
(*Obair/Fostaíocht*)

Iomad na lámh a bhaineann an cath.
The abundance of hands wins the battle.
(cf. Many hands make light work.)

Is geall le sos malairt oibre.
A change of work is as good as a rest.

Ní fhaightear saill gan saothar.
There is no fat without labour.

Is trian den obair tús a chur.
A third of the work is to begin.

Gnáthamh na hoibre an t-eolas.
Knowledge comes from doing work.

Fear gan saothar fear gan saol.
A man without work is a man without a life.

Molann obair an fear.
Work praises the man.

Youth and Age (*Óige agus Aois*)

Mol an óige agus tiocfaidh sí.
Praise youth and it will prosper.

Ní thagann an óige faoi dhó choíche.
You are only young once.

Ní féidir ceann críonna a chur ar ghualainn óig.
You can't put a wise head on a young shoulder.

Tabhair póg (nó: béal) do bhean óg agus cluas don tseanbhean.
Give the young woman a kiss and an ear to the old woman.

Ní peaca an tseanaois; ní suáilce an óige.
Old age isn't a sin; youth isn't a virtue.

Cead a chos ag an ógfhear, cead a súl ag an ógbhean agus cead a chinn ag an seanfhear.
A young man may go where he likes; a young woman may look at whom/
what she likes; and an old man may think what he likes.

Is fada ón óige a beatha agus is fada ón seanfhear a uaigh.
The young long for life; the old man longs for the grave.

Lá seilge don ógfhear agus lá reilige don sean.
The young man must appoint a day for hunting; the old man a day to die.

*An té nach bhfaigheann breith ar fhéile na hóige—beidh breith ar aiféala
na seanaoise aige.*
The person who does not enjoy the bounty of youth will enjoy the
remorse of old age.

Latin Proverbs
(Seanfhocail na Laidine)

Dimidium facti qui bene coepit.
Tús maith leath na hoibre
Well begun is half done.

Vultu ridere invito.
An chuma is fearr a chur ar dhrochmhargadh.
To make the best of a bad job.

Uno saltu duos apros capere.
An dá éan a mharú leis an urchar céanna.
To kill two birds with the one stone.

Arcem ex cloaca facere.
Míol mór a dhéanamh de mhíoltóg.
(Don't) make mountains out of molehills.

Nondum omnium dierum sol occidit.
Bíonn súil le muir ach ní bhíonn súil le huaigh.
Where there is life there is hope.

Pares cum paribus facillime congregrantur.
Aithníonn ciaróg ciaróg eile.
Birds of a feather flock together.

Quail rex, talis grex.
Cad a dhéanfaidh mac an chait ach luch a mharú.
Like father, like son.

Cedendum multitudini.
Ní neart go teacht le chéile.
There is strength in numbers.

Non e quovis ligno fit mercurius.
Cuir síoda ar ghabhar agus is gabhar i gcónaí é.
You can't make a silk purse out of a sow's ear.

Hurculi quaestum conterere.
Ní dhéanann an mochóirí glic airneán an bhroic.
Do not burn the candle at both ends.

Quandoque bonus dormitat Homerus.
Ní bhíonn saoi gan locht.
Even Homer nods.

Omnia vincit amor.
Ní féidir an grá a shárú.
Love conquers all.

Necessitas caret lege.
Múineann gá seift.
Necessity knows no law.

Beati possidentes.
Is minic gur fearr agam ná liom.
Possession is nine points of the law.

Variatio delectat.
Beagán de mhórán a mhéadaíonn do dhúil.
Variety is the spice of life.

Noscitur ex sociis, qui non cognoscitur ex se.
Inis dom cé hiad do chairde agus neosfaidh mé duit cé tú féin.
Tell me who your friends are and I tell you who you are.

Tempora mutantur, nos et mutamur.
Athraíonn an saol agus tagann athrú orainn leis.
Times change and we change with them.

Si vis pacem, para bellum.
D'fhear cogaidh comhaltar síocháin.
If you desire peace, prepare for war. (Vegetius)

Si vis amari, ama.
An té a bhfuil grá ina chroí, gheobhaidh sé grá!
If you wish to be loved, love. (Seneca)

Audentis fortuna iuvat.
Níor chaill fear an mhisnigh riamh.
Fortune favours the bold. (Terence)

Russian Proverbs
(Seanfhocail na Rúisise)

Русские Пословицы

Бабушка гадала, надвое сказала.
Thuar Mamó an dá rud. (Is féidir an dá chiall a bhaint as a bhfuil ráite.)
Granny prophesised two things.
(No one can know for certain.)

Беда никогда не приходит одна.
Nuair a thagann cith, titeann bailc.
It never rains but it pours.
(lit. Problems never come alone.)

Брюхо сыто, да глаза голодны.
Tá do bhéal níos mó ná do bholg. (Tá do chíocras níos mó ná do ghoile.)
Your eyes are bigger than your belly.
(i.e. Do not be greedy.)

Доверяй, но проверяй
Bíonn creideamh ag laoch ach ní creideamh caoch.
Have trust, but make sure,
(i.e. It is good to trust others, but we should also keep an eye on things.
A similar Arab proverb advises: Trust in the Lord, but tie up your camel!)

Дурная голова́ нога́м поко́я не даёт.
An té ar a bhfuil ceann lag, ní mór cosa láidre bheith air.
A person who has a weak head must have strong legs.

Рука руку моет, вор вора кроет.
An té a thabharfadh gal domsa, thabharfainnse gal dósan.
You scratch my back and I'll scratch yours.
(lit. One hand washes another / one thief covers for another thief.)

Рыбак рыбака видит издалека.
Aithníonn ciaróg ciaróg eile.
Birds of a feather flock together.
(lit. One fisherman sees another fisherman from far off.)

Семь бед—один ответ.
Ó loisc tú an choinneal, loisc an t-orlach!
In for a penny, in for a pound!
(lit. Seven transgressions—one punishment.)

Старость—не радость и смерть не свадьба.
Ní sonas seanaois, ní bainis bás.
Old age isn't happiness and death isn't a wedding.
(i.e. However bad old age is, death is worse.)

Старый друг—лучше новых двух.
Níl aon chara mar sheanchara.
There is no friend like an old friend.
(lit. An old friend is better than two new friends.)

Сытый голодного не разумеет.
Ní thuigeann saibhir daibhir.
A rich man never understands a poor man.
(lit. The well-fed person does not understand the hungry person.)

Работа не волк, в лес не убежит.
Is lá eile amárach.
The work can wait for another day.
(lit. Work is not a wolf; it won't run away into the forest.)

Polish Proverbs
(Seanfhocail na Polainnise)

Polskie Przysłowia

Bez pracy nie ma kołaczy.
Mura gcuireann tú ní bhainfaidh tú.
Without work there won't be supper

Gość w dom—Bóg w dom.
Is ionann aoi sa teach agus Dia sa teach.
Guest visiting the house—God visiting the house.

Gdzie zgoda tam i siła.
Ní neart go teacht le chéile.
Together we stand; divided we fall.
(lit. Where there is agreement/unity there is strength.)

Jak sobie pościelesz, tak się wyśpisz.
Cóirigh do leapa i gceart agus beidh codladh sámh agat.
As you made your bed so you must lie in it.

Kowal zawinił a Cygana powiesili.
Fuarthas an gabha ciontach ach crochadh an ghiofóg.
The blacksmith was guilty, but they hanged the Gypsy.

Kropla do kropli i będzie morze.
Is mór iad na beaganna i dteannta a chéile.
Drop after drop, there will be an ocean.
(cf. Every little helps.)

Ładnemu we wszystkim ładnie.
Fiú i ngiobail, bíonn an áilleacht go hálainn.
A pretty person looks well in anything.

Lepszy rydz niż nic.
Is fearr leath ná meath.
A half a loaf is better than none.
('*rydz*'—red pine mushroom)

Lepiej późno niż wcale.
Is fearr go mall ná go brách.
Better late than never.

Nie mów „hop", póki nie przeskoczysz.
Ná maraigh an fia go bhfeice tú é!
Don't count your chickens before they're hatched.

Nie wszystko złoto, co się świeci.
Ní théann an áilleacht thar an gcraiceann.
Not all that glitters is gold.

O umarłych mówi się dobrze, albo wcale.
Ní mhaslaítear na mairbh.
Speak well of the dead or not at all.

Ten się śmieje, kto się śmieje ostatni.
Is fada an gáire an gáire deiridh.
He who laughs last, laughs the longest

Wolnoć Tomku w swoim domku.
Is máistir gach duine ar a theach féin.
An Englishman's home is his castle.

Wszędzie dobrze, ale w domu najlepiej.
Níl aon tinteán mar do thinteán féin.
There is no place like home.

Wszystko dobre, co się dobrze kończy.
An cluiche deireanach an imirt.
All's well that ends well.

Gdy sowa przychodzi na piknik u myszy, to nie po to,
żeby wziąć udział w wyścigach w workach.
Nuair a thagann an ceann cait go picnic na luch,
ní hé chun páirt a ghlacadh sna sacrásaí.
When an owl comes to a mouse picnic,
it's not there to take part in the sack races.
(*Tomasz Banacek*, American TV series)

To, że sukienka jest z czerwonej satyny, nie znaczy,
że łatwo ją zdjąć.
Fiú má tá an gúna déanta den sról féin, ní chiallaíonn sin is go bhfuil sé
éasca a bhaint.
Just because a dress is red satin doesn't mean it comes off easily.
(*Tomasz Banacek*, American TV series)

Dwanaście dobrych koni i srebrne świeczniki nie zatrzymają
opadów śniegu w Białymstoku.
Ní stopfaidh dhá chapall déag agus coinnleoirí airgid
an titim sneachta in Bialystoc.
Twelve good horses and silver candlesticks won't stop
the snow from falling in Bialystock.
(*Tomasz Banacek*, American TV series)

Nawet tysiączłotowy banknot nie potrafi stepować.
Ní féidir fiú nóta bainc de mhíle szloty cniogrince a dhéanamh.
Even a thousand szloty note can't tapdance.
(*Tomasz Banacek*, American TV series)

Italian Proverbs
(Seanfhocail na hIodáilise)

Proverbi Italiani

L'ospite è come il pesce, dopo tre giorni puzza.
Bíonn aoi cosúil le hiasc, tar éis trí lá bíonn boladh bréan uaidh.
A guest is like a fish: after three days it stinks.

A caval donato non si guarda in bocca.
Ná féachtar ar fhiacla an chapaill a bhronntar.
Don't look a gift horse in the mouth.
(A horse's age can be judged by inspecting its teeth, and so it is poor form to investigate the age of a horse that has been gifted to you!)

A chi fa male, mai mancano scuse.
An té a bhíonn i mbun an oilc, bíonn leithscéal faoi láimh i gcónaí aige.
He who does evil is never short of an excuse.

Aiutati che Dio t'aiuta.
Is gaire cabhair Dé ná an doras don té a bhíonn ar a dhícheall.
God helps those who help themselves.

Belle parole non pascon i gatti.
Ní mhaireann na bráithre ar bhriathra.
Fine words butter no parsnips.
(lit. Fine words don't feed cats.)

Chi dorme non piglia pesci.
Is leis na mochóirí an lá.
The early bird catches the worm.
(lit. Those who sleep don't catch any fish.)

301

Cuando l'amico chiede, non v'è domani.
Nuair a iarrann cara (gar) ort, níl aon amárach ann.
When a friend asks, there is no tomorrow.

L'amore vince sempre.
Bainfidh an grá mullach na sléibhte is airde amach.
Love conquers all.

La semplicità è l'ultima sofisticazione.
Is í an tsimplíocht an tsofaisticiúlacht is airde.
Simplicity is the ultimate sophistication.

Mangia bene, ridi spesso, ama molto.
Bia breá, gáire minic, agus an grá gan teorainn!
Eat well, laugh often, love much.

Nulla nuova, buona nuova.
Dea-scéala gan aon scéala!
No news is good news.

Quando finisce la partita il re ed il pedone finiscono nella stessa scatola.
Nuair a chríochnaítear an cluiche, cuirtear an ceithearnach agus an rí sa bhosca céanna.
When you finish the game, the king and pawn end up in the same box.
(cf. *Téann an fear saibhir chun na reilige i gcóiste agus an bochtán i gcairt ach itheann na cruimheanna iad araon*—The rich man goes to the cemetery in a coach and the poor man in a cart, but the maggots eat both.)

Una cena senza vino e come un giorno senza sole.
Béile gan fíon, lá gan ghrian!
A meal without wine is a day without sunshine.

Noi non potemo avere perfetta vita senza amici.
Ní saol é go cuideachta carad.
We cannot have a perfect life without friends.

German Proverbs
(Seanfhocail na Gearmáinise)

Deutsche Sprichwörter

Aller Anfang ist schwer.
Bíonn gach tús crua.
Every beginning is difficult.

Des Teufels liebstes Möbelstück ist die lange Bank.
Ná cuir ar an mhéar fhada aon rud gur féidir a dhéanamh inniu.
Do not put off till tomorrow what can be done today.
(lit. The Devil's favourite piece of furniture is the long bench.)

Wer rastet, der rostet.
An té nach mbogann, tagann am mheirg air.
He who rests grows rusty.

Aus Schaden wird man klug.
Is maith an t-oide and teip.
We learn from our mistakes.

Das Billige ist immer das Teuerste.
An rud is saoire is daoire sa deireadh.
What is cheap costs more in the long run.

Erst denken, dann handeln.
Is fearr féachaint romhat ná dhá fhéachaint i do dhiaidh.
Look before you leap.
(lit. First think, then act.)

Eile mit Weile.
Déan deifir go measartha mall!
Make haste, but slowly!
(i.e. It is good to do what needs to be done speedily and effectively but we equally should not forget to take pleasure from the beauty and joys of life.)

Kümmere Dich nicht um ungelegte Eier.
Ná maraigh an fia go bhfeice tú é.
Don't count your chickens before they've hatched.

Morgenstund hat Gold im Mund.
Is leis an mochóirí an lá.
The early bird catches the worm.
(lit. The morning hour has gold in its mouth.)

Taten sagen mehr als Worte.
Ní mhaireann na bráithre ar bhriathra.
Actions speak louder than words.

Übung macht den Meister.
An cleachtadh a dhéanann máistreacht.
Practice makes perfect.

Dienst ist Dienst und Schnaps ist Schnaps.
Más obair – bí ag obair, más sult – bain sult as!
Work is work and play is play.
(i.e. There is a right time and a right place for everything)

French Proverbs
(Seanfhocail na Fraincise)

Proverbes Français

Qui vivra verra.
Is maith an scéalaí an aimsir.
Time will tell.
(lit. He who will live will see.)

La barbe ne fait pas le philosophe.
Is minic nach ionann cófra agus a lucht.
Don't judge a book by its cover.

Chacun voit midi à sa porte.
Eala gach éan gé ag a mháthair.
Every mother thinks her own gosling a swan.
(lit. Everyone sees midday at their (own) door.)

Petit à petit, l'oiseau fait son nid.
I ndiadh a chéile a thógtar na caisleáin.
Rome wasn't built in a day.

Chacun sent le mieux où le soulier le blesse.
Tuigeann gach duine cá luíonn an bhróg air.
Everyone knows best where the shoe pinches him.

De mauvais grain jamais bon pain.
Cuir culaith shíoda ar ghabhar agus is gabhar is gcónaí é.
You can't make a silk purse out of a sow's ear.
(lit. You never get good bread from bad grain.)

Il faut être deux pour danser le tango
Bíonn beirt ag teastáil don tangó.
It takes two to tango.

L'essentiel du courage c'est la prudence.
Is fearr rith maith ná drochsheasamh!
Prudence is the better part of valour.

Les volontés sont libres.
Beatha duine a thoil.
People are free to choose.

Qui m'aime aime mon chien.
An té a bhuailfeadh mo mhadra, buaileadh sé mé féin!
Love me, love my dog!

Si jeunesse savait, si vieillesse pouvait.
Ní féidir ceann críonna a chur ar ghualainn óig.
It's impossible to put a wise head on young shoulders.
(lit. If youth knew how and if old age could.)

Tel père, tel fils/Telle mère, telle fille.
Cad a dhéanfaidh mac an chait ach luch a mharú.
Like father, like son/Like mother, like daughter.

Je crains l'homme de un seul livre.
Ní léann leabhar amháin (agus ní píobaireacht aonphort.)
Fear the man of one book.

A vaincre sans péril, on triomphe sans gloire.
Sa rud nach bhfuil baol ná dua níl glóir ná bua.
To win without risk it to triumph without glory. (Corneille)

Qui craint de souffrir, il souffre déjà de ce qu'il craint.
An té atá eaglach roimh fhulaingt atá ag fulaingt den eagla cheana.
He who fears suffering is already suffering that which he fears. (La Fontaine)

La vérité vaut bien qu'on a passé quelques années sans la trouver.
Bíonn blas níos fearr ar an fhírinne má thógann sé tamall le teacht uirthi.
Truth is more valuable if it takes you a few years to find it. (Renard)

Spanish Proverbs
(Seanfhocail na Spáinnise)

Proverbios Españoles

Atar a los perros con longanizas.
Madra a cheangal le hispíní.
To tie the dogs with sausages.
(i.e. to waste money/effort on a useless endeavour)

Cuando seas padre, comerás huevos.
Agus tusa i d'athair, íosfaidh tú uimheacha.
When you become a father you will eat eggs.
(Only the head of the household was fortunate enough to be able to eat
eggs. This is said to children, and is a version of 'when you live in your
own house you can make your own rules.')

Entre la espada y la pared.
Idir an claíomh agus an balla.
Between the sword and the wall.
(i.e. faced with hopeless alternatives. cf. Between a rock and a hard place/
Between Scylla and Charybdis.)

Quien a buen árbol se arrima, buena sombra le cojiba.
An té atá faoi chrann maith, bíonn sé faoi scáth maith freisin.
Who is beneath a good tree is well shadowed.
(i.e. It is important to surround oneself with good friends and influences.
cf. One takes one's colour from the company one keeps.)

El que se fue a Sevilla, perdió su silla.
An té a théann go Sevilla, tá a chathaoir caillte tr'éis dó filleadh.
He who went to Seville lost his chair.
(Once you relinquish something (a possession, your place in a line, etc.), you lose it. This has its origins in the fifteenth century, when Archbishop Alonso de Fonseca went on a trip to Galicia for Church-related matters, and ceded his power to his nephew while he was away. On his return, the nephew refused to return him to the post.)

El que busca la verdad, corre el riesgo de encontrarla.
An té a lorgaíonn an fhírinne, bíonn an baol (i gcónaí) ann go nochtfaidh sé í.
Who searches for truth risks finding it. (Isabel Allende)

En realidad las cosas verdaderamente difíciles son otras tan distintas, todo lo que la gente cree poder hacer a cada momento.
Is iad na rudaí go gceapaimid bheith éasca a dhéanamh am ar bith a bhíonn i ndáiríre ina ndeacrachtaí móra (dúinne).
In reality, the things that are truly difficult are those that people believe they can do at any time. (Julio Cortázar)

No hables a menos que puedas mejorar el silencio.
Ná bí ag caint ach amháin má cheapann tú gur féidir leat an ciúnas a shárú.
Don't speak unless you can improve on silence. (Jorge Luis Borges)

La sabiduria nos llega cuando ya no nos sirve de nada.
Tagann an ghaois nuair bhíonn sé ró-dhéanach.
Wisdom comes to us when it's already too late. (Gabriel García Márquez)

Acknowledgements

My sincere appreciation and thanks to the late Dr David Sowby, whose scholarship and patient examination have been indispensable and central in all areas of the work. Also I would like to thank everyone at New Island Books, in particular editor Justin Corfield for all his patience and very salient advice, and also Dan Bolger and Edwin Higel.

I am grateful to Tania Stokes for illustrating the proverbs so beautifully, to Caoimhe Ní Bhraonáin for casting her eagle eyes over my Irish, and to Alejandra Mateo and Rosario Campos Olivares for providing some Spanish proverbs.

I hope you enjoy this collection of Irish Proverbs and that you can carry it with you while you are travelling on holidays, going to school or college, or off to your daily grind. Why not learn one or two new proverbs every week because '*is i ndiaidh a chéile a tógadh na caisleáin*' and '*nach mór iad na beaganna i dteannta a chéile*'? Before you know it you'll be '*chomh ciallmhar le Sola féin*'!

Go n-éirí leat!

—Garry Bannister